Hidden Treasures
in
Your Field

Leon Patillo

(Mr. Leon)

ISBN 978-1-64458-758-4 (paperback)
ISBN 978-1-64458-757-7 (digital)

Christian Faith Publishing, Inc.
832 Park Avenue
Meadville, PA 16335
www.christianfaithpublishing.com

Printed in the United States of America

Introduction

Last year I was searching for one theme that would be woven through the Gospels of which, undeniably, love was at the base of them all. In my investigation, I discovered a lot of contributing themes that were hidden just beneath the surface, so I thought I would get out my spiritual shovel and start digging. And when I did, I discovered *hidden treasures.*

The way this book is set up will be very easy to digest. On days when you just need a pick me up, I pray that this book will get your mind off of your depression or challenges, inspire you, and may it reveal something relevant right before your eyes.

Just the other day I was challenging myself concerning the next music release that entails a *new genre of music* for our kids and grand-kids. I was so overwhelmed by the challenge that I forgot who the real source of my success was. I started flipping through this manuscript, and I ran into a scripture that said, "Ask me anything in my name, and I will do it." At that moment, it was as if heaven was assisting me in my faith and giving me just the encouragement I needed right then! And because of that one thought, all the weight of the project got shifted. I still had to do the work, but it's as if the huge door in front of me that seemed so heavy had hands on them, helping me to push. So that's what you will experience, as the ground around you becomes unearthed and you will find *hidden treasures in your field.*

A book of Memoirs.

Structure

I will present you with a scripture and then a commentary. You'll know the commentary by the heading (LP) beside it. The verses I have picked are ones that seemed to strike a chord with me. Also, I recently discovered the ERV (Easy Reading Version). It breaks the verses down to more of a digestible language. There is nothing worse than to read a whole chapter and then start scratching your head wondering, *What did He say?*

I'm starting in the book of Luke because that was the first book that seemed to really pop out at me. I love following our Savior's example of storytelling, so I have *lots* of stories, experiences, and testimonials woven throughout.

I pray this experience will help you see a fresh new side of Jesus and find *hidden treasures in your field.*

Luke 1

Her name was Elizabeth. Zechariah and Elizabeth were both good people who pleased God. They did everything the Lord commanded, always following his instructions completely. But they had no children. Elizabeth could not have a baby, and both of them were very old.

—Luke 1:5–7

(LP) Bear, Past Bearing Years

You can do everything the Lord has asked you to do and still have challenges in your life all the way up to old age. But like in this case, God saw Zach and Lizzie's heart and granted their request, even *past bearing years*, which is a great reminder that even though you may be past bearing years, God is still able to make you bear!

When I moved to Las Vegas four years ago, I thought it was to retire. The housing market was at an all-time low, and there were buffets on every corner. I said, "Now *this* is the place to retire!" But what I didn't know was that this city had the highest dropout rate in the whole country! So I thought maybe I could redirect the attention of the kids in this city toward music and the arts. Many schools as you know have cut out the art programs because of budget restraints.

With that in mind, I started an organization called the SING Foundation (Sowing Into Next Generation) whose goal is to change the future of the next generation through music and the arts. My first project was a contest where singers could compete and whoever won would sing with me on my next CD. During the planning stage of this overwhelming endeavor, I met Rich, the GM of Findlay Toyota (who at the time of this writing has recently passed away). When I shared my thoughts and vision with him and his staff, they all got excited and wanted to help in redirecting the hearts and lives of these eight-to sixteen-year-olds. So, since the beginning of my journey, Findlay Toyota has been our sponsor.

Well, to my surprise, there was a lot of young talent in this town. They showed up at Findlay Toyota where we held the contest by the hundreds. When the judges tallied all the scores, it yielded six equally talented contestants. So we gave all six first-place status, and they sang with me on my CD *You Can Begin Again*. I say that to say this—even though you may be on your back nine. As long as you've got breath in your body, ideas in your head, and a passion in your heart, God can use you *past bearing years*!

Haggai 2:9 says it best: "The Glory of this present house will be greater than that of the former, saith the Lord. And in this place, there will be peace, saith the Lord." Just like me, I bet you've seen it over and over again in your life that when you get to the end of something, a new beginning begins! That is truly a *hidden treasure in your field*. And I thank John and Liz for their example of how God can use someone later, even much later in life.

> Then, on the right side of the incense table, an angel of the Lord came and stood before Zechariah. When he saw the angel, Zechariah was upset and very afraid. But the angel said to him, "Zechariah, don't be afraid. Your prayer has been heard by God. Your wife Elizabeth will give birth to a baby boy, and you will name him John. You will be very happy, and many others will share your joy over his birth. He will be a great man for the Lord. He will never drink wine or beer. Even before he is born, he will be filled with the Holy Spirit.
>
> John will help many people of Israel return to the Lord their God. John himself will go ahead of the Lord and make people ready for his com-

ing. He will be powerful like Elijah and will have the same spirit. He will make peace between fathers and their children. He will cause people who are not obeying God to change and start thinking the way they should. (Luke 1:11–17)

(LP) Families Can Be Revived

The part that speaks to me, and I'm sure to some of you traveling parents, is the middle of verse 17, where it says, "He will make peace between fathers and their children." It's good to know that even at this late date, God can cause a healing between parent and child. No matter how much guilt is heaped upon us because of our shortcomings, we shouldn't sit around wallowing in twenty years ago of what should have been or could have been. That time has passed, but if we still have breath in our bodies, we can start a new relationship right now.

According to this scripture, that was a part of John's call. To me it's like a reminder from the Holy Spirit that we should be led by Him to guide us into all truth. And the truth is that our Lord can cause a *family to be revived.*

My father and I didn't have the best relationship, and it took many years for my heart to respond appropriately in that area. We sometimes tend to point out all the bad traits in somebody and don't realize that in most cases there is more good about them than bad. Every day is a new day with new possibilities that will move us away from the darkness and the things that try and rob us toward the glorious light of a different mind-set and a renewed spirit, which can reverse what we never thought possible—*hidden treasures in your field.*

"Zechariah said to the angel, "How can I know that what you say is true? I am an old man, and my wife is also old" (Luke 1:18).

(LP) Don't Let Your Doubt Interfere with God's Plan

Even Zach had some doubt issues, even after an angel's appearance. The angel must have been like, "Say what? Have you ever had in the history of your life an angel from heaven appear before you?" But the angel was cool and stayed focused and gave Zach his credentials.

> The angel answered him, "I am Gabriel, the one who always stands ready before God. He sent me to talk to you and to tell you this good news. Now, listen! You will not be able to talk until the day when these things happen. You will lose your speech because you did not believe what I told you. But everything I said will really happen."
>
> Later, Zechariah's wife Elizabeth became pregnant. So she did not go out of her house for five months. She said, "Look what the Lord has done for me! He decided to help me. Now people will stop thinking there is something wrong with me." (Luke1:19–25)

(LP) Dreams Can Come True

There comes a time, eventually and in God's timing, when what He has promised, comes to pass. It may be later in life, especially if it's got something to do with a monumental event.

Here is a story that I thought might ignite your mind and encourage you toward the edge a bit!

In 2009, Kim Dinan lived in a great city, owned a home, and had a good job. Life was nice. But she knew deep down that something was missing. She'd always dreamed of traveling the world. At one point, back in college, she wanted to write for a living. But somewhere along the way her dreams had ended up on the back burner. So she hatched a plan.

For the next three years Kim and her husband saved every penny and sold all their stuff. In May 2012 they set out to travel the world with all their remaining possessions strapped to their backs. "There was definitely a point where I wondered what we were doing, if we hadn't both completely lost our minds," said Kim. "But, of course, that wasn't what we wanted."

Today Kim and her husband travel the world full time, and Kim has turned her love of writing into a career. Since bucking the cubicle for a life of travel, they've trekked the tallest mountains in Nepal and descended into the world's deepest canyon in Peru. Kim has walked solo across Spain and driven a rickshaw three thousand kilometers through India.

Today she lives the life she used to only dream about. "Life is an adventure now," she said. "I've truly come to believe that if we can find the courage to do the things that make us feel most alive, we not only do ourselves a favor but the world too!"

I share this story with you to stir up the gift that is within you. There may be a sleeping giant of possibilities waiting to arise. Don't let age be a deterring factor, young or old. It didn't for Zach and Liz or this couple above. Find your passion and bless the world with it. *Your dreams* are *hidden treasures in your field*.

> "Your relative Elizabeth is pregnant. She is very old, but she is going to have a son. Everyone thought she could not have a baby, but she has been pregnant now for six months. God can do anything!" (Luke 1:26, 37).

(LP) God Can Do Anything

Anytime, anyone of us become discouraged, these words should be on the tip of our tongue—"God can do anything!"

I have recently been reading a book by Mark Batterson called *The Circle Maker*, which is a *New York Times* Best Seller. The book makes an emphasis on prayer. I believe, like Mark, that there is a dimension you tap into when you saturate your dreams and visions with prayer. Like when a plane takes off. You feel the bumps on the runway and pressure as you lift off. But in a short time, you feel a breakthrough as you soar above the clouds to the designated altitude. Life can go through those same exact steps. But all along the way, you know your God is carrying you to heights that you've only dreamed of. Because every step of the way, you keep saying, "My God can do anything!" I use the airplane analogy because an average 747 commercial airliner weighs 987,000 pounds at takeoff, which really boggles the mind, and yet it flies. So getting up and going again doesn't even compare to that gravity-defying stunt.

> "Mary said, 'I am the Lord's servant. Let this thing you have said happen to me!' Then the angel went away" (Luke 1:38).

(LP) Every Word Is True

What a great attitude to have, and notice because of it, no repercussions like Zach. It's a great plus to life if we can cultivate an attitude of letting go and letting God. Sometimes there is a distrust because God hasn't come through in the time we thought He should. Mary was the youngest in the group but responded like the oldest. I always say in my concerts that the revival we are all anticipating is going to come through the youth because they don't have as many issues as us older folks have. Some have become cynical, and others believe they have arrived. But the young are filled with so much awe and wonder that they believe just about anything we tell them. Oh, if we could be that way again. To believe every word that comes from the mouth of our Heavenly Father. Hollowed would truly be Thy Name...again.

> "God has helped Israel—the people he chose to serve him. He did not forget his promise to give us his mercy. He has done what he promised to our ancestors, to Abraham and his children forever" (Luke 1:54–55).

(LP) Your Road Has a Life-Changing Intersection

God's faithfulness has always been amazing to me, even after so many unfaithful moments on my part. It teaches us to stay the course because we never know what life God has predestined for us. I always remind the singles that if they stay on the road of their assignment, they will eventually intersect the person of their prayers. And as a sidenote, not only does that happen in romance but in business too.

For example, Mom and Dad always had foster children in our home when I was growing up. So when I left the Santana band, I wanted to do the same thing. My friend and agent Bill Reed knew the owner of a foster homes organization out of Sacramento, California, called Koinonia Foster Homes. When I heard that homeless children needed a home, I really felt I could assist them in accomplishing that task. I worked with them for more than twenty years, right up until the time the CEO retired. Our combined efforts have created thousands of homes for less fortunate children.

I remember in the early days, we were scratching our heads and wondering how we were going to attract parents for these little ones. Then Miriam, the CEO of the company, came up with the idea of taking a cruise so we could have a concentrated time to flush out some ideas. She said it could be part business, part vacation. It sounded good to everybody except me. I had been on cruises before, and the picture I was imagining was a multitude of couples all hugged up and looking at me, a single man, like "Too bad you ain't got nobody." But then they told me that they would pay for the trip. So I said, "Hmmm, you know, a cruise don't sound too bad."

It ended up being a seven-day cruise to Mexico, and as I predicted, it was everything out of a couple's fairy tale. I was anxious to get on with the business part of the trip, but two days had gone by and nobody was interested in meeting.

To help with my boredom, I found a piano toward the aft part of the ship, just outside of a nightclub, and I started writing a song called "Serve You." The lyrics came easy to me because of my readings from Ephesians 5 about how the man was supposed to serve his wife.

During my moment of creativity, the dolphins started jumping up past the windows. I could faintly hear calypso music playing in the background and couples were passing me all hugged up sipping on drinks with umbrellas in 'em. I said to myself, "This is a horrible place for a single man to be." I stopped playing and whispered a little two-word prayer, "Surprise me!" You laugh, but that's a legitimate prayer!

And as I begin playing again, a Filipino guy walked toward me, sat down, and immediately started singing. Even though he had a good voice and all, I whispered back up to heaven, "Lord, not that kind of surprise!"

Then from a distance, I saw this gorgeous lady coming toward me with a big beautiful smile. And just like out of a movie scene, she looked like she was walking in sl-o-o-o-o-w motion, smiling and nodding her head up and down ever so slowly and flopping her short hair from one side to the other. I didn't see a ring on her finger, so I started smiling back and shifted my voice into a lower range. But as she got closer, she cut away and sat next to my new Filipino friend. I thought, *Oops, that's probably her husband*. But to my delight, after a few songs, they got up to leave and introduced themselves as brother and sister! *Yes!* Well, as you can imagine, it was on from there. I turned my head toward the skies and said, "Now that's the kind of surprise I'm talking about!"

It's a joy to announce that we have been together at the time of this writing for more than two decades—long time for a musician. But she is truly one of God's *hidden treasures*.

I'm telling you this story because it was all about being on my assignment with Koinonia Foster Homes that this romantic inter-section happened. Just like Zach and Liz, God fulfills His prom-ises, even a small prayer like "Surprise me." So I say to you singles, "Cruise, baby! There may be a *hidden treasure* waiting for you.

> "And so the little boy John grew up and became stronger in spirit. Then he lived in areas away from other people until the time when he came out to tell God's message to the people of Israel" (Luke 1:80).

(LP) Springs in the Desert

I don't know about you, but when I have desert times in my life, I have to keep reminding myself that it's a preparation for a greater thing. Of course, it's more noble, like John, to do it proactively. But even if it's forced upon us, the end result is still the same. You're tried and tested for the Master's use!

A desert experience may be needed so He can pull your arrow back for a season so when He lets go, the whole earth will see you blazing across the sky.

For me I'm always thinking of ways to have my soul's purpose be expressed. This is my first attempt at a book, but I don't want you to think that I just woke up yesterday with this idea. I have been having these desert thoughts running through my mind for a long time now. And to be honest, some days I feel like I have invincible moments and some days I feel like a dry sponge in the desert. It's on sponge days that I remember what Mel Gibson alluded to in the middle of directing *The Passion of the Christ* that he even felt lost in what he was trying to achieve. To hear such an experienced professional admit sponge moments gave me longer legs to run toward my goal.

I thought that my life's expression was only through music but come to find I had *hidden treasures* right up under the surface in the forms of videos, TV hosting, pastoring, teaching, mentoring arts programs for kids, and now this book. When it's all said and done, it equals *"springs in the desert."*

So as you unearth the ground around you, I hope this form of expression from your brother will assist you in that quest. When we think about various directors and producers that brought us entertainment like *The Ten Commandments, ET, Hunger Games, Alien Invasions*, and Disneyland, I'm sure their story about how it all came about had a desert experience attached to it somewhere. When your desert comes, you might want to sing,

"Spring up O well, within my soul.
Spring up O well, and make me whole.
Spring up O well, and give to me.
That life…abundantly!"

Luke 2

Joseph registered with Mary because she was engaged
to marry him. (She was now pregnant.)

—Luke 2:5

(LP) Jesus Understands the Fatherless

It is a fact that Jesus had his earthly father for a season, and then there was no more mention of him. That's why Jesus can identify with a child growing up without a father. Every successful ball player gives the same shout out, "Hey, Mom!" There are multiple stories of how the mother struggled to raise this special child and then they grow up and become superstars.

I too was raised partially with my dad in the home until he passed away at the young age of forty-seven from military-related injuries. Immediately, everything shifted to Mama, like the financials and the weight of raising us kids. A lot of nights I would pass my mom's room and see her on her knees. And I believe that the father-less side of Jesus sympathized with her plight and answered her in ways that only she knew was the Lord. Knowing Mama Doll like I did, I'm sure that her prayers were for the children. I know this from all the foster children that were running around our house during my childhood.

Personal:

I continue every day to redeem what the cankerworm stole. I make this promise to God and to myself what Mama Doll and Papa Artist invested in me will rise from the dust to honor them. Souls beyond belief, every nation and tongue, will worship at His feet. The young and the old, the black and the white, every other nationality and religion will hold Jesus in the highest honor because there is none like Him in all of world—the maker of all things, the sustainer of all people. If naysayers know Him or not, His mercy is still causing them to live, move, and have their being. Thank you, Moms, Dads, and Grandparents, for following Christ's lead and extending your love to those without parents. You are the *hidden treasures in our field*.

> "So they went running and found Mary and Joseph. And there was the baby, lying in the feeding box" (Luke 2:16).

(LP) You Become What You Feed On

It's interesting how the baby was placed in a box that the animals were eating from. It's a subliminal message that we should somehow be feeding on Jesus. That's why the scriptures say in Isaiah 55, "Come, all you who are thirsty, come to the waters; and you who have no money, come, buy and eat!"

The birth of Jesus was an amazing occurrence that has been etched in time. Feast on the food that the scriptures give. Draw strength from His challenges and calling. Marvel at all prophesies and events that went in to Him being destined to come to this planet. Be amazed at His humility and the miracles surrounding the people He touched. Feast on that and you will have enough to eat until His return.

One of the first suggestions I got after leaving the Santana band for the call was to stay in God's word. After leaving the group, it was all I had to do because I didn't have a job. It was a scary time, of course, but it was an adventure because I never knew what God had for me just around the corner.

Before leaving the group, I bought a little house in Oakland, California, on a beautiful tree-lined street with at least a car-length worth of space between houses. I liked this property because in the backyard the former owners had built what looked like a man cave.

Of course, that's why I bought it, with thoughts of turning it into a recording studio.

Just to show you how important it is to feed on God's word: on a visit to San Francisco one day to see my mother who lived in the Haight-Ashbury district, I stopped off at a lookout spot on top of Pacific Heights. This spot at night was known to be lover's lane, but during the day, buses and lots of tourist would stop and take in the view of the whole city.

On this particular day, I took my Bible up there to pray and see what God wanted me to do with my house or man cave. I had thoughts of having Bible studies in the home, which was a noble thought. But beautiful Christian music dripping on the lost and dry souls seemed like a great thought too. But my dilemma was what did the Lord want out of me first. Well, I did a very desperate thing in that I put my hand in the Bible and flipped it open.

It opened to the book of Proverbs, chapter 24, and my eyes landed on verse 27, which said, "Put your outdoor work in order and get your fields ready, after that, build your house." Boy, was I ecstatic at that answer! God's word not only gave me direction but a place to put my focus and passion.

With the limited funds that I had, I started working on this project frantically.

I even called my uncle who was a self-taught carpenter. I felt extremely close to this uncle because I was named after him. My dad thought so much of my mom's sister's husband that he gave him that honor. Of course, I found out later that my dad did this because they couldn't have children so I became like their surrogate son.

I take you down this memory lane to make a point about feeding on God's Word. "He knows all of the seasons that we will go through, up or down, we still must look to you" as the song says. His word is *hidden treasures in your field.*

> "They brought Jesus to Jerusalem so that they could present him to the Lord. It is written in the law of the Lord: "When a mother's first baby is a boy, he shall be called 'special for the Lord'" (Luke 2:22–23).

(LP) Kids Should Be Exposed to Church

Presenting the children is a great practice for parents. It is a great teaching tool for the kids as well—pointing out God's involvement in their life. When we think along those lines, the children have a fighting chance and are made aware of the spiritual component behind their lives.

I have always felt special, but I didn't really know that it was from God. Nothing to boast about, just a reality check so I can stay mindful of my assignment.

Mom was Baptist, dad was Methodist, and when they didn't feel like going to church, they would send me down to the local Catholic church where I became an altar boy. And because of that, I always tease that my theology is all mixed up! But it gave me a great overview of different denominations that has weaved its way right into my present life.

My time in Dad's Methodist church was sort of a relief because, unlike my mom's thousand-member church, Dad's was much smaller and more intimate. I had even tried out to be the piano player for my mom's church, but I wasn't quite up to speed for them yet. But at my pop's place, they were hungry for someone, anyone, with my type of skills, especially since they were trying to attract more young people.

As soon as I started playing there on occasion, all the youth from the neighborhood started to come! Looking back, it felt a little like the first *Sister Act* movie with Whoopi Goldberg. Every time I'd play, here they'd come.

Mrs. Leonard, the organist for the senior choir, had so much faith in me that she gave me a key to the church so I could practice the organ. Now the organ was really a challenge to my coordination because I had to have four things going at the same time—right hand on the upper keys, left hand on the lower keyboard, foot pedals for the left foot, and a volume control pedal for the right foot. *Whew!* I thought many days, *Why did I sign up for this challenge?*

I remember the first Sunday I was set loose on the congregation to handle all its musical needs. It came off okay, but it really gave me a greater respect for you women who multitask so flawlessly!

Looking back, I guess this *firstborn* came with a lot of *hidden treasures* that God could use, and I thank my parents for exposing me to church and their spiritual guidance in my life. Because of it, I have energized and been energized by more denominations than I ever thought possible.

> "Jesus's father and mother were amazed at what Simeon said about him. Then Simeon blessed them and said to Mary, 'Many Jews will fall and many will rise because of this boy. He will be a sign from God that some will not accept'" (Luke 2:33–34).

(LP) The Grandparent-Grandchild Connection

As a parent, can you imagine hearing that from somebody, especially a stranger? What a way to kick off a relationship with your newborn!

Even in the case of Jesus, there was adversity surrounding his life. Even His mom and dad heard good news and not so good news. It is in the fabric of being human that some suffering will come, but thanks be to God who has overcome the world. So when adversity comes, we put on our full armor and stay ready for whatever we have to encounter.

Of course, as you know, only 4 percent of the millennials go to church now. My suggestion is, and has been, that you grandparents bring your grandchildren to church! You may not be able to persuade your children right now, but once the grands go to Sunday school or summer Bible week, they will get excited about church and start spreading that excitement to their parents. Then it's just a matter of time before it motivates your children to come check it out.

I was watching a show on TV called *Little Big Shots* with host Steve Harvey. It showcased youngsters with extraordinary gifts. The day I was watching, a little grammar school girl came on to sing. And, as is Steve's habit, he would interview the child before they would do their act. When He asked the grammar school girl about the first song she learned to sing, she blurted out, "Jesus, Jesus, Jesus, there's just something about that name. Kings and kingdoms shall all pass away, but there's something about that name." I was shocked that they didn't cut that part out of the show! But as I thought about it, it came to me that a lot of us have been praying for revival in our land and throughout the country—praying that something miraculous would happen to touch mankind in a way that would draw hearts toward the heavens and each other again. And as I watched this little girl, it was as if I was experiencing it in real time—a holy moment coming through a youth. It also occurred to me that this is why, systematically, the dark side has been trying to knock off our little ones.

It started with Moses, then Jesus, and now, this suicide epidemic that we are experiencing motivated by bullying, which in my investigation has a lot to do with self-esteem issues among our children. What's interesting about the little girl's performance was that when she was asked who taught her that song, she pointed to her grandmother in the audience! Wow! *Grandparents*, you are our *hidden treasures*."

> "Jesus said to them, 'Why did you have to look for me? You should have known that I must be where my Father's work is.' But they did not understand the meaning of what he said to them" (Luke 2:49–50).

(LP) Father's Work: Our Key Assignment

This is a key phrase for us faith-based people to remember: "Where My Father's work is." Where is your Father's work? Is it being a single mother to your kids or an only Christian in the workplace? To know one's assignment is one of the greatest knowings you can have.

Again, that's why we as parents and grandparents should school our kids on spiritual-type subject matters as early as we can. It could save them from running into a lot of unnecessary walls or setbacks.

I was privileged to sing at the twenty-fifth anniversary of Crossroads Church in Yuba City for my friends and Pastors Jim and Marilyn Clark. A week before we came, we were discussing details concerning having their children sing with me. During this conversation, Pastor Marilyn was talking about her children's class that she teaches. She mentioned that there was a little five-year-old boy who she felt had already figured out what his God-given *assignment* was. She said he had a very special heart like Martin Luther King or Sister Teresa, one bursting through with love for others.

One day the little boy asked Sister Marilyn if she loved him. And her instant reply was, "Yes, of course! And Jesus loves you too." When he heard that, the little boy jumped up in her lap, hugged her, and said, "I know that I am loved...because bugs love to bite me!" Oh, if we could only be as simple and gentle as children, heaven would come that much closer to earth.

My work is my *Father's work* toward the little ones in Vegas and other select cities across this great land. I believe it's why I keep getting new songs, producing videos, and performing in concert. It's all about *His work*.

Our *Father's work*, as I have come to realize, starts with an itch in your heart that God put there to confirm His call. That's why we have such a drive or passion in a particular area. It may not be what someone else might think is the *Father's work*. But you stay on the road God has got you on—and you'll find an invaluable *hidden treasure*.

> "Jesus went with them to Nazareth and obeyed them" (Luke 2:51).

(LP) Rules Create Protection

If the Son of God allowed Himself to be subject to parental guidance, even more reason for us to be. There are reasons for rules. If we didn't have any, this planet would be in an even more chaotic state.

Say for instance, when a light turns red, we should stop, right? But what if some would say, "I don't really *feel* like stopping." Not only is that dangerous for that person and their passengers, but it puts everybody else in that environment at risk.

Parents play an irreplaceable role in the lives of their children. This vital relationship positively impacts a child's physical, mental, and emotional well-being. The right of parents to maintain a strong involvement in their children's lives has been continually upheld by Supreme Court doctrine.

1. Children who have parental support are likely to have better health as adults.
2. Students with involved parents tend to earn higher grades, have better social skills, and are more likely to graduate and go on to post-secondary education.
3. Children are more likely to be socially competent and have better communication skills when they have parents who are sensitive to their needs and emotions.
4. Teens who are monitored by their parents are one-quarter as likely as teens with "hands-off" parents to smoke, drink, and use drugs.

Their practices and principles is a natural *protective* measure—even after our parents have gone on to be with Jesus.

Luke 3

*I baptize you in water, but there is someone com-
ing later who is able to do more than I can. I am
not good enough to be the slave who unties his san-
dals. He will baptize you with the Holy Spirit and
with fire.*

—Luke 3:16–17

(LP) Shift Our Celebrity to the Source

I love how John takes his celebrity and puts the focus on Jesus. It is
the challenge of every life to shift the credit to where credit is due.
You can never go wrong when you give God the glory.

In years past I had a season of being a part of and ministering
to a group of Hollywood stars. In an attempt to be transparent with
you, even though I run the risk of your judgment, I had two dwell-
ings that I felt, even when I was purchasing them, that they were
going to be comfortable for my elite friends to possibly have Bible
studies in.

The first was a penthouse in Glendale, California. Then a year
later, a twelve-thousand-square-foot house in Bel Air. And as I sus-
pected, it was the perfect fish hook. It was spearheaded by the late
great Motown producer, Frank Wilson, who after his salvation, had
a God-driven goal to see Hollywood covered in the blood of Christ.

Most of our discussions were about how to let our light shine
in our industry and how to get the word out to this dark and needy
world. I can truly say that every one of us became a positive product of those meetings. We watched our narcissistic personalities get
transformed into a God- first attitude. Singers added Gospel songs

to their set or made some reference about our Lord in concert. Actors made suggestions for more family-oriented language in movies and on TV. Some directors and producers even decided to make outright spiritual and inspirational films.

I'm also happy to report, as I have taken a recent inventory, that all careers have hit a new level of exposure and success. In fact, the spark continues even today through my good friends Karen and Jim Covell and the *Hollywood Prayer Network.*

Shifting our celebrity to the Source is a safe and humble muscle for all of us to keep developing. It's also a tremendous *hidden treasure.*

> "'He will separate the good grain from the straw, and he will put the good part into his barn. Then he will burn the useless part with a fire that cannot be stopped.' John said many other things like this to encourage the people to change, and he told them the Good News" (Luke 3:17–18).

(LP) We All Need an Encourager

Useless is one word I pray I never hear coming out of the mouth of our Father. I would rather be called useless in my fame in this world than to be useless to God and His Kingdom because this life is like a vapor. I was a teenager a few months ago, now I'm on the back nine of my life. And I already know what I'm going to be asked at the gate: "Who did you bring witcha?"

My training as a young Christian was due to a lot of concerned people. But one special man in my life, Pastor Danny Di Angelo, who in those days was the youth pastor at Glad Tidings Church in San Francisco, the place Richard brought me to be fed the Word. Pastor Danny caught up with me just after my return to the faith, and we had a glorious time talking about the Lord and our ultimate assignment to assist people into the arms of Jesus.

Of course, we liked to eat too so we found a restaurant two blocks from the church. It was a place that sold bean pies. Ohhh, I can taste them now! I didn't know if I was excited about hooking up with Pastor Danny or stuffing my face with those sweet-potato-type pies. But his effect on my life was like John the Baptist—a gentle direction when I was confused and a strong rebuke when rebellion tried to dominate my heart. He was my *hidden treasure* that manifest at the perfect time.

It's always important to have an encouraging friend, even someone that may not agree with you all the time but has a word that they can share from their own experience to motivate you to rise in that exact moment in your life challenge. Even me as a God-fearing man, I sometimes feel like I can handle life and all of its complexity with just me and the Lord. But that's not how Jesus sent out His disciples—He sent them out two by two.

We should also keep our eyes open to become an encourager. There is nothing sweeter than "the feet of those who bring good news!" To become someone's *hidden treasure in their field*.

> "When all the people were being baptized, Jesus came and was baptized too. And while he was praying, the sky opened, and the Holy Spirit came down on him. The Spirit looked like a real dove. Then a voice came from heaven and said, 'You are my Son, the one I love. I am very pleased with you'" (Luke 3: 21–22).

(LP) Three in One

It's exciting and historical all at the same time that we have a passage in scripture that captures all three of the Godheads in the same place—the Father, the Son and the Holy Spirit. All three distinct individuals with different functions but accomplishing the same purpose. When I think about the state of our country, we need this corporate model—a wonderful example of powerful forces working together and going after one goal. On the political front, we should pray that the nations of the world will use their power for unifying and not for division, taking their power and influence to assist in the needs of mankind.

I'd also like to mention that verses 23 to 38 are dealing with the genealogy from Adam to Joseph, which shows us that it was all a plan, with different people having a part during their era to achieve, like the *Three in One*. If anyone of these people would have been out of place or unwilling to cooperate, the whole lineage line would have been put in jeopardy. Our lives today have a profound effect on the future. Working together to achieve our most important goals is the baton that we pass from generation to generation. It is *thee hidden treasure in our field.*

Luke 4

Jesus answered, "But the Scriptures also say, 'You must not test the Lord your God." The devil finished tempting Jesus in every way and went away to wait until a better time.

—Luke 4:12–13

(LP) Don't Let Anything Stop You from (Go)-ing

I love how with every appeal from the dark side Jesus used scripture to combat it. It might have taken place audibly, but like most of us, that sort of static is always being presented to our minds. So we have to be strong in the Lord and in the power of His might, which I identify as the helmet of salvation. You've got to know in your mind that you are saved, no matter what all the visuals suggest, even concerning our flaws. In spite of them, we are still God's children washed in His blood, guided by the Spirit, made in the image of God, and on our way to heaven one day!

This whole passage from 16–30, Jesus reads the Isaiah 61 scripture and explains its fulfillment in Him, then proceeds to talk about past miracles that had been performed, not favoring Israeli people. In a sense, He was saying, "Don't just get stuck on your kind of people, when what you have inside of you from God should be offered to everyone in need." Now this sort of talk got everybody mad, but it was the Lord's way of trying to expand their ministry's reach. It was the "Go ye therefore" scripture of the Old Testament. So Matthew 28 was the sequel for it and a continuing theme. When you think you have nothing to do in your life and boredom sets in, there is so much for us to get involved in that there should never be a dull moment or a time when were just sitting around thinking about woe is me. That's another thought that the enemy is trying to plant in our mind. I heard someone say the other day, "We don't really retire, we get re-fired!"

We can feed the poor, minister to prisoners, pray for the sick, and just outright proclaim God's Kingdom to those who will listen—coworkers, family, and friends. And even if you're bedridden, you can still use your mind to effect someone, especially now through social media. But also know that we will have the most resistance in our own homes, especially around people that know us intimately. Don't freak out, it happened to Jesus too.

> "Jesus went to Capernaum, a city in Galilee. On the Sabbath day, he taught the people. They were amazed at his teaching because he spoke with authority" (Luke 4:31–32).

(LP) You Are Worth More Than You Think

"Spoke with authority"—so it comes up again. I believe that when you have had some experiences from all that life has taught you, you become a person of influence, a person of authority. I notice it all the time around the kids I mentor. I gave them an example of their worth the other day, and they told me that it was something that they'll never forget.

The group that day were the eleven-to sixteen-year-olds. The question I asked them was, "How much do you think you're worth?" One said, "Fifty dollars!" and the whole class went, "Whoa!" Another said, "One hundred dollars!" Everybody whispered back, "one hundred dollars, that's a lot of money!" One yelled out, "Five hundred dollars!" and everybody started laughing.

I told them, "The truth, guys, is that you're worth $44,000." They all looked at me like I was a crazy man. Then I had them to take out their cell phones and make a calculation. We started with, how much their parents had spent on them from the time they were in the womb till eleven years old. And by the time we added up diapers, milk, doctor bills, gas, clothing, schooling, books, outings, toys and such, it came out to forty-four thousand. Then I mentioned that in today's economy, that should be doubled. I told them, "So you're truly worth $88,000." Of course, I had previously sat with my accountant Lidia B. and that's exactly what she had calculated.

The youngsters of today are unaware of their worth, and that could be a contributing factor in why there are so many suicides among our youth. Of course, the majority of my group are singers and dancers and some have chosen to make their living from that art form. As their mentor and person of *authority* in their lives, it is my duty to make them aware of their value so that managers, agents, and promoters don't take advantage of them. So when they are asked to perform, they feel good about what they've charged. And as I always tell them, give the fans more than what they paid for.

Another lesson I've learned over the years is that when you think the kids are not listening, don't make your judgment based on their body language. In that same class that day, there was a young boy, Connor, who was a straight-A student. But this day he seemed like he needed some medication.

We generally have our sessions in the board room at Subaru of Las Vegas because the facility is centrally located between all the different areas where the kids live. My wife talks with the parents in one room, and the kids and I are just down the hall.

At the end of the class I told the kids to go give their parents a *big* hug and say, "Thank you, Mom and Dad, for spending eighty-eight thousand dollars on me!" Well, to my surprise, the young boy who was rolling around in his chair and gazing out the window ran over to Renee (because his parents hadn't come yet) and told her word for word everything we discussed in the class! I was blown away when Renee told me. All the time I thought he was bored and was not paying attention! I guess our job is to plant the seed, and no matter how they respond, God will use the seed in a positive way in their lives. The children are an excellent place to invest our years of experience and *authority*. It is a *hidden treasure* that will get their young tender lives kicked off with more substance and stability!

"The people were amazed. They said to each
other, 'What does this mean? With authority and
power he commands evil spirits and they come
out.' And so the news about Jesus spread to every
place in the whole area" (Luke 4:36–37).

(LP) He Is the Resurrection and the Life

Another case of authority. To me this puts Jesus in a league of
His own. But even with this authority, His main concern was to
relieve this man from his suffering. What still amazes me about our
Savior is that, this is exactly why He came to this planet—to save us!
That one act on the cross did it all. And if I have any problem getting
up after a fall, I remember that He has the authority to call me up
and out, like He did the day He broke free from the tomb.

We hear it a lot nowadays about life after death. One scripture
we can always depend and defend our heart with is, "I am the resurrection and the life. He who believes in me, though he were dead,
yet shall he live."

Take authority today, Lord, and speak into my life the areas that
so want to serve you and submit to you, oh Lord. I need you to speak
into them, Jesus. This is a time when all of us that have something to
contribute for good should rise up in His authority and do just that.
With your leadership, your insight, and foresight, we can reshape the
desolate future predicted for our children and our children's children.

We know that you will be coming back soon, so help us to send
out the message across the world. Jesus is coming. Jesus is coming.
Every eye shall see him, from ABC to NBC to CBS to Fox, CNN,
and WB. All the cameras will be pointed toward the sky as the sound
of thousands upon thousands of angels' wings will be fluttering over
the earth. And Jesus Himself will be riding on a white horse, as the
voices of the saints past and saints present will be shouting, "Holy,
Holy, Holy, is the Lord God of Host! And the nations will bow before
the King of kings as all of creation…will be set *free!*"

We think we have seen great movie effects during our time but
hold on because you ain't seen nothin' yet—because the greatest of

spectacles has not even begun, because "Eye hath not seen, nor ear heard, or has it entered into the heart of man the things that God has prepared for those who love Him, and are called in accordance to His purpose." Unleashed will be the *hidden treasure* Himself.

> "The next day Jesus went to a place to be alone. The people looked for him. When they found him, they tried to stop him from leaving. But he said to them, 'I must tell the Good News about God's kingdom to other towns too. This is why I was sent.' Then Jesus told the Good News in the synagogues in Judea" (Luke 4:42–44).

(LP) Compelled to Go!

This is the reason why I passed the baton to Charles D. and family in 2009. It was a direct order from the Lord—that the Good News about God's Kingdom needed to be spread to other towns. I have always been a part of His worldwide mission, and I was honored to become re-engaged again, even "past bearing years."

We had a church called the Rock House in Long Beach, California, from 1998 to 2009. Our claim to fame is that we eventually ended up in the *Queen Mary* ship that was docked in the Long Beach Harbor of California. The experience of meeting my wife on a cruise was the motivation for the experience we called "A Church on a Boat," which I thought was a good slogan. Just like life, we're just floating through.

It was a pleasant experience, and our congregation really loved coming to church. The only drawback was that, with pastoring and all, it didn't give me a chance to reach out to any other parts of the planet. And as time went by, I felt like I was hiding away from a big needy world. Then that itch that I talked about became overpowering toward evangelism. So after a session with the board, it was agreed that I should go back out and complete my mission on the frontlines. The most difficult thing was to break physical ties with so many that I had grown to love and hangout with at least once a week. But through the years we have still been able to stay in touch, and it's funny because when we begin to talk or text, we just pick up from where we last left off, as if no time has passed. Charles, his wife Teresa, and my assistant Debra continue the church experience and are calling it The Gathering.

When I returned on the road again, I ran into so many people who told me how my music had impacted their lives, how after all these years, they were still standing because of the message in the music. It was such a confirmation then, and still is now, as we unveil this new book and inspirational music for the youth. And I pray that this book will cause the same effect on the souls of you who need to know that you have *hidden treasures in your field.*

Luke 5

When Jesus finished speaking, he said to Simon,
"Take the boat into the deep water. If all of you will
put your nets into the water, you will catch some fish."
—Luke 5:4

(LP) Prepare Your Nets, the Fish Are Coming!

This is a great analogy of what our part is and what God's response will be. There is so much water on this planet that fish are waiting in droves to be scooped up in our nets. Suffice to say, the bigger the net or the more nets we have in the water, the more likely we will be to catch a big haul.

There are a lot of opportunities offered us in this life. And when I'm discouraged sometimes, I think about these fishermen that were hanging out with life Himself and still had to be instructed on how to throw in the net and bring in the haul.

Case in point below:

> Simon answered, "Master, we worked hard all night trying to catch fish and caught nothing. But you say I should put the nets into the water, so I will."
>
> The fishermen put their nets into the water. Their nets were filled with so many fish that they began to break. They called to their friends in the other boat to come and help them. The friends came, and both boats were filled so full of fish that they were almost sinking. (Luke 5:5–7)

This is my prayer today, Lord, that you would continue to make us a net-breaking attraction, especially to the youth. Continue to strengthen our nets so they will be so strong, that nothing human or consequential could break them, that we won't become so proud that we won't solicit the help needed to accomplish such a great call and honor.

Prepare Your Nets:

I was telling you about my man cave up in Oakland, right? So my uncle Leon and I cut wood and ate hamburgers for a month straight. It also gave us a chance to catch up on our relationship.

My routine was to drive from Oakland over the Bay Bridge down Fell Street through the Golden Gate Park, out to Forty-Sixth Avenue, which was right near the beach; pick up my uncle; back over to Oakland; work all day; then drive him home late afternoon. This is what we did, five days a week. I tried to get him to stay overnight some nights, but he didn't want to leave his wife, Edith, alone, which I thought was cute.

Neither one of us knew much about soundproofing a room, but we knew when we got through, I would be able to write and record songs that would create a net. It was good in another way too for Unc and I to spend some much-needed time together. He was truly the closest to a dad I'd ever had, given that my father had passed away from military-related injuries fifteen years before. And it wasn't long after that project that Uncle Leon went home to be with Jesus.

When the project was finished, I spent most of my days praying, writing, and recording in this new studio, preparing for a *huge haul*.

The Actual Catch Zone:

After about six weeks a husband-and-wife team out of Sacramento, California, Pastor Lewis and Mary Neely, got word of my departure from Santana. They convinced me to come and do a concert for them. They explained that they had a youth outreach in their church called Warehouse Ministries, because, literally, it was in a warehouse. They told me that kids of all ages came to their concert series on Saturday nights to listen to contemporary Gospel music.

I agreed to do a concert for them, but I explained that I only had about thirty minutes worth of inspirational-type music. Mary was so hyped about the possibility of me coming, even with a thirty-minute set that she scheduled me within the month.

Witnessing Two Master Fishermen in Action!

When I arrived, which was hours before the concert, there was already a line forming around the building. Suddenly, I got sick to my stomach because I had never performed these songs live, especially for kids half my age!

You see how all along God was setting me up for my future call?

The night of the concert, they gave a rousing introduction, including highlights from my career and former affiliation as lead vocalist from Santana. As I approached the stage to a standing-room-only explosive reception, I felt more butterflies in my stomach than ever before! When I said, "Hello," the whole audience said *hello* back in unison! Then the entire place went silent and became tuned to each song and the emotion behind it. Their responses at key places in the songs reinforced that observation. The song I closed with was "How Can I Begin to Thank You," which in this environment had the perfect words and expression that we all felt about our newfound Savior. Since my set was so short, Pastor Lewis asked me to do that song again! And like the first time, everyone stood and applauded, which was honoring but a little embarrassing too!

Pastor Neely came back up and gave a contemporary-style message and appeal for those who wanted to make an affirmation of faith. Again, I was shocked to see so many hands go up. It seemed like half the room responded. At that moment, I flashed back through all the prophesies that had led me to that moment. And in an instant, I knew what I was on this planet to do—*to catch souls!* And, yes, Pastor Neely was the Jesus prototype of how to accomplish that goal.

When he got through, he asked me to come back and do an encore. So I did the "Thank You" song again! What was so funny was that the attendees gave the same exact response as the other two times! LOL! It was the first time in my career that I had sang one song three times in the same concert!

That *soul-catching* experience was where I got hooked—and has been with me all these years. It taught me that what comes out of the mouth of the Lord is irresistible bait. And my brother, my sister, when we get to heaven and see all the catch, it will take all eternity to greet them all. They will be the *hidden treasures in your field.*

> "Jesus said to Simon, 'Don't be afraid. From now on your work will be to bring in people, not fish!' The men brought their boats to the shore. They left everything and followed Jesus" (Luke 5:10–11).

(LP) Realignment of Our Assignment

Even though the apostles' secular work before their call was very successful, Jesus let them know that with their new call they would still be catching—but not fish. In fact, He was pretty specific: *"From now on your work will be to bring in people, not fish."*

Again, one basic foundation for us to stand on is Matthew 28:19, "Go ye therefore and teach all nations, baptizing them in the name of the father and the Son and the Holy Ghost. And lo, I will be with you forever and ever. Even until the end of the age." When we get confused about our call, this one scripture will help realign and reassign us.

Because of my secular background, every once in a while I'll reminisce about the what-ifs— what if I had stayed with the group, what if I had pursued a rock-and-roll music choice as a saved person, what if I was still single instead of married these two decades. What if? Moses seemed to struggle with that at the burning bush. What-if questions. It can happen to anyone, and that's why we need a realignment Scripture that gives us a firm direction from our Savior, like the one He gave Simon.

Every day is not going to be a mountaintop experiences, but the valleys He takes us through prepares us for the next big climb. To oppose His call would be like a forty-year loop in the desert, round and round and round we go, fearful and doubtful that we could even accomplish His call on our lives.

Even after the nation of Israel saw an overpowering deliverance from their captors, an ocean opened up right before their eyes with manna, quail, and water flowing consistently in the desert. They never took each miracle as a realignment opportunity.

I guess, like us sometimes, we forget to look back and take inventory of all the miraculous that has brought us to this very moment. So thank God for His *realignment of our assignment*: "From now on your work will be to bring in people, not fish." A key *hidden treasure*.

> "Jesus said, 'I want to heal you. Be healed!' Then he touched the man, and immediately the leprosy disappeared. Then Jesus said, 'Don't tell anyone about what happened. But go and let the priest look at you. And offer a gift to God for your healing as Moses commanded. This will show people that you are healed'" (Luke 5:13–14).

(LP) Old School and New School Working Together

I love how Jesus included the authority of Moses, who was truly their respected leader. Even though Jesus's teachings was a bit radical. On this occasion, He reminded them of their tradition. This was genius *old school-new school* thinking.

I love it when I go to contemporary churches and experience spirited praise, then somewhere in the set they begin to sing an old hymn. Even if it's done in a contemporary style, the spirit of the song brings in a certain maturity that only words and melodies from that era can do. It's like grabbing an ember from the past that has weathered the storms of time and is still standing and beckoning us back to our first love.

I had the privilege of singing at the Seventh Day Adventist Church in Spoken Valley this year. It was mostly a traditional church in its nature. But they allowed me to bring a more contemporary flare to our time together, *which was old school-new school* at its best. But to bridge the gap, I did the Lee Greenwood song "Proud to be an American." Toward the middle of the song, everyone began standing, singing and waving their arms in honor of our military, past and present.

I got that from our Lord in how he dealt with this healing. Both his disciples and the Sanhedrin had to appreciate how He handled that one. I know the two expressions can coexist because my *Live Experience* album was crafted in that way. And is still the number-one-selling live album of all time. It is the *hidden treasure* in both fields!

> "But the news about Jesus spread more and more. Many people came to hear him and to be healed of their sicknesses. Jesus often went away to other places to be alone so that he could pray" (Luke 5:15–16).

(LP) Isolation Inspires Motivation

The PR about Jesus was his drawing power. It was the people spreading the word because Jesus said, "Don't tell anybody about these miracles." When you tell people not to, that's the first thing they want to do! Good strategy.

We also see what made him so charismatic and irresistible. He was spending isolated time with the Father. This is a pattern that, when followed, will make greatness flow from, even an ordinary person.

Everyone will agree that a change of environment is healthy. We recently went to Hawaii for a series of concerts. I'm so thankful for the cell phone photo technology. It can really capture a moment. The other night as I was drifting off to sleep, I pulled up a few pictures from that tour and was instantly transported to the island.

It's that way in prayer too! The moments that are spent with the Lord in different locations, even if it's on top of the roof where you work, it seems to spark a whole new freedom in your prayer language.

Of course, a place like Hawaii would be monumental. But even when you go on prayer walks around the neighborhood or through the park, you come home refreshed and revived.

Psychologically, it opens you up to be able to interact with the Savior anywhere you are. That, my friend, is truly *hidden treasures in your field*.

> "They lowered the mat into the room so that the crippled man was lying before Jesus. Jesus saw how much faith they had and said to the sick man, 'Friend, your sins are forgiven'" (Luke 5:19–20).

(LP) Go the Extra Mile to Love

When we go after Jesus with such passion and determination, it reminds us and shows our Savior that he is the only answer for our problems. I think of the woman with the issue of blood. She had nowhere else to turn. She had to touch Jesus or die.

Along those lines, there is a hospital in Arizona whose emphasis is on creating a healing environment. A report by Laurie Eberst says:

> When a new hospital is being planned and built, much of the focus is often placed on how many beds it will house, where each department will be located, how many it will employ and the bottom-line cost of the project.
>
> This is not necessarily the case for Catholic Healthcare West's (CHW) Mercy Gilbert Medical Center in Arizona, which opened its doors in June, 2006. While these considerations were important to the company's plans for the hospital, the leadership team worked hard to ensure that the facility was built to reflect, in

every way possible, a healing environment. One that helps patients feel safe and comfortable, one that reminds staff why they chose healthcare as a line of work.

Mercy Gilbert Medical Center pride themselves on being a Healing Hospital, not only as a healing facility, but also as a healing culture. And these are 3 key components in the hospitals philosophy. (1) A Healing Physical environment. (2) The integration of work design and technology. (3) A culture of Radical Loving Care. Also in their mission statement, it says, "We have learned that providing a loving, compassionate aesthetically pleasing environment promotes healing.

I know it sounds a little bit like a commercial or an endorsement, but I must take my hat off to these people for trying to do something outside the box. And no doubt they have had healings where God stepped in and did something supernatural that no one could explain. And I don't say that to put the physicians down but to say, "Thanks, guys, for going the *extra mile to love* and have compassion on those that are hurting and even dying in some cases. You are a true *treasure* in my book."

> "The man immediately stood up in front of everyone. He picked up his mat and walked home, praising God. Everyone was completely amazed and began to praise God. They were filled with great respect for God's power. They said, 'Today we saw amazing things!'" (Luke 5:25–26).

(LP) Amazing!

After a concert, that's the buzz I love hearing—*amazing*!

I had the good fortune on my last tour to perform at a senior home facility in Spokane, Washington. There was a mixture of dif-

ferent people from all cultures and ethnicities. I even asked if anyone was from the baby boomer generation—born between 1946 and
1964. They all begin to laugh and say, "Maybe our kids." Some of
them were in wheelchairs, some were even tied to an oxygen tank,
but many were active and were ready to dance! The next day the
director of the facility told me that everyone was commenting that
they had the greatest time and still could sense holiness in the air. My
word back to her was "*Amazing!*"

I was in New Orleans one time, and a beautiful fourteen-year-
old girl walked into the concert with scoliosis, a disease that makes
the back shape like a *S* or a *C*. She seemed to have a great attitude and
was smiling as if nothing was wrong. Well, as the concert continued,
I took time to reach out to those who were suffering from physical
issues. I did as I always do. I started singing the first song I wrote
when I rededicated my life to the Lord again, "We Must Believe."

About halfway through the song, I sent up a prayer for the sick
along the lines of the miracle that Jesus performed on the boat, calm-
ing the winds and the waves, and I paralleled it with the fact that
Jesus could speak to our physical, mental, and psychological issues
in the same way and command them to leave. I even told those who
were suffering to raise their hands and those around them to put
hands on them or hug them and pray for them.

We continued to sing as we all felt this soothing warmth in
the air. And right on time something wonderful happened for the
little fourteen-year-old fan. As we were praying, I later found out
that people heard the girl's bones cracking as she began to stand up
straight for the first time in her life. All I could say was, "*Amazing!*" I
got word weeks later that when the little girl went back to school on
Monday, the whole school was *amazed* at the miracle that had happened to her. When she was asked about her healing, she said, "Jesus
healed me at a Leon Patillo concert!"

I still get goose bumps when I think of being that close to a
God-miraculous event. Now you see why I had to title this book
in this way. How would I have known before the concert that God
had this *hidden treasure* waiting for this precious little one? But just
beneath the surface, there it was! Like putting on goggles and going

underneath the ocean, you experience a whole other existence of life. That's what's going on in the spirit realm all the time—a *hidden treasure* just beneath the surface waiting to manifest! If we could have the faith to challenge ourselves to press in more in prayer and intercession, we would hear this word ringing in the air—*Amazing*!

> "Jesus said to him, 'Follow me!' Levi got up, left everything, and followed Jesus. Then Levi gave a big dinner at his house for Jesus. At the table there were many tax collectors and some other people too" (Luke 5:27–29).

(LP) A Christ Atmosphere Is Disarming

I have always loved how Jesus was able to get audience with such diverse people—and to mix with them in a way that had them curious about his mission. There's just something about that man, as is stated below:

"It is the sick people who need a doctor, not those who are healthy. I have not come to ask good people to change. I have come to ask sinners to change the way they live" (Luke 5:31–32).

I love how Jesus had a heart for struggling people, like in verse 32, "I have come to ask sinners to change the way they live." I don't know if you're feeling it like I am right now, but when someone says, "Change the way you live," it's not that easy! It's one thing for us to make a confession of faith, but a whole other thing to change patterns and habits. But His presence is *disarming* because when His Spirit comes into a room, or into your life, molecules change. Even commonality between people start to happen. I've even seen it from church to church. Couples may be arguing in the parking lot, but as soon as they walk into the sanctuary, the *Christ atmosphere* takes over.

I will be the first to admit that I was found and then I got lost again for a season. That can happen in any field, no matter if you are a pastor or a policeman. Time of introspection has to be taken, and if issues come up that have been there for a long time, like since childhood, some counseling may need to be put into the mix. One thing is for sure, if we yield to His Spirit, like a child would in the arms of her mom or dad, there is comfort, there is peace because the Ultimate Love is wrapped around you.

This is part of a counseling story, as told by Lynne Shall cross, and how the counselor changed the *atmosphere.*

"I don't have to talk with you, and you can't force me to talk with you."

Not the ideal way for a counseling session to begin, but John Sommers-Flanagan didn't let his young client's rebuff stop him. Instead of fighting back with a clever retort however, he simply told the client she was 100 percent right.

"I can't force you to talk about anything," said Sommers-Flanagan, an associate professor in the University of Montana Department of Counselor Education. "It's completely your choice. In fact, if I ever try to force you to talk about anything, I hope you tell me because I'm totally not interested in forcing you to do anything."

After a short silence, Sommers-Flanagan went on to explain how he likes to work with clients in counseling.

"You know, counseling is really weird," Sommers-Flanagan told the young woman. "We're total strangers, and yet, somehow, you're supposed to walk in here, sit down, and tell me about important stuff in your life. Well, I really don't expect that. Instead, what I'd like to do is to begin by telling you what I've been told about you. I think that's fair because I've gotten information from your file and from your intake counselor. So I'm just going to tell you what I've heard, and you can tell me if it's right or not."

This type of start to the counseling relationship isn't out of the ordinary for Sommers-Flanagan, who coauthored with his wife Rita Sommers-Flanagan in *Tough Kids, Cool Counseling: User-Friendly Approaches with Challenging Youth*, published by ACA.

"Nearly every week, I meet with youth and young adults ages sixteen to twenty-four and nearly all the students with whom I meet don't want to meet with me," he says. "This makes the initiation of the counseling process very difficult."

I mention this article to point out that your visit to a place of help like this is not only a stretch for you but for the counselor too! And in this case, the orator made a point of creating a *Christ atmosphere.*

In my early days of being counseled, my instructor taped all our sessions. I might have felt a little intimidated while I was in his office. But listening back to it, in the privacy of my own home, was *disarming* and healing for me.

If more of us brought a *Christ atmosphere* to our environment, I think a lot more could be accomplished between family members, husband and wife, parent and child, and even between boss and coworkers.

And my friend, if you are having any doubts about "help" concerning your struggles. Let me tell you with certainty that counseling is a *hidden treasure in the field.* You get answers to things that all humans deal with. You even find out that you're not as weird as you thought. And that many struggle with the same issues as you do. *Counseling* is another part of body health, like working out or drinking water! And if your counselor brings a *Christ atmosphere* to the session, even better.

This sort of attitude is why Jesus was able to be a spiritual magnet at the tax collector's house. He brought His A game into a situation where most holy people don't even want to hang out. So I encourage you too. Bring a *Christ atmosphere* into whatever environment you find yourself in and see how many will be attracted to the beautiful heart of Jesus that we have grown to love. He is the *hidden treasure in your field.*

> "You always put new wine into new wineskins. No one who drinks old wine wants new wine. They say, 'The old wine is just fine'" (Luke 5:38–39).

(LP) Controversy Attracts

I love how Jesus used controversial subjects to explain his points. In some circles, if you even bring up wine, they think you're backslidin'. Controversy done right, with the intent to attract a non-saved ear, could be a *hidden treasure.*

In the early years of contemporary Christian music, a lot of us took the heat for having certain instruments in the church like electric guitars, drums, and loud speakers. Of course, the youth loved it, and truthfully, I believe that was God's plan—controversy done right, like a wholesome debate or a nonviolent protest.

For us Christians, we should look for contemporary ways to attract the non-saved ear. If one is creative, there are limitless ways for that sort of appeal through social media. And for you grandparents, if you come up with an idea that would be controversial but don't know how to do it on the computer, ask you grandchild!

I wrote a song for one of our presidents, based on the campaign slogan he was using at the time. The song was so controversial that within a week a national news organization flew from New York to do an interview with me. The song and the interview reached more homes nationwide than I ever dreamed possible. And the lyrics were very specific about our nation getting back to faith in God.

You say, "Yeah, Leon, that's easy for you. You write songs for a living. Well, you can do something that's close to home for you too, like buying a gift for someone at work that you have a hard time communicating with, with a card filled with love and care for the other coworker. That sort of *controversy attracts*. It could be an instant fix, or it may take a minute for your love to sink in. But the seed is planted. And according to our Savior, love still reigns supreme and this is just one example. If you sit and listen in your time of prayer, God will give you your special way to bring attractive controversy.

Luke 6

Stand here where everyone can see. The man got up and stood there. Then Jesus said to them, "I ask you, which is the right thing to do on the Sabbath day: to do good or to do evil? Is it right to save a life or to destroy one?"

—Luke 6:8–9

(LP) Kind Words Heal!

This is what happens after I sing "Flesh of my Flesh" at the concerts. I generally have the couples stand up and renew vows to each other. It seems to be the right thing to do, given the state of our families today. In fact, I have heard over and over again that some of the couples were on their way to the divorce court; but after heartfelt, *kind words* are spoken, starting with the husband, the dark wall of failed communication comes crumbling down.

It's not only encouraging for the couples, but it's also awesome for those who are looking on, especially their children and grandchildren, who in most cases, have never heard those *kind of words* spoken to each other before.

Just like the scripture above, "Jesus had the man to stand, and in the eyes of everyone there, He performed a miracle." After the concerts, many couples say the same thing. By standing up in front of the whole congregation, it's like putting their hands to the plow again. And they agree that the new vow is just what was needed to reignite their commitment. Wow, who could have ever guessed that a new vow could be such a powerful *hidden treasure*!

My brother-in-law Willie and his wife, Marlie, just renewed their vows. It was their fiftieth anniversary. They had their priest and me to pray. And both of us had nothing but *kind words* to say about these too.

The same was true about my friend Rich Abijian, GM of Findlay Toyota! When we celebrated his home going, we had to make a video. Because there was so many well-wishers. With nothing but praise for my Christian brother, I can truly say that many of us are *still* reaping the benefits of his labor. "Then Jesus said to them, 'I ask you, which is the right thing to do on the Sabbath day: to do good or to do evil?'"

It's my prayer along with yours that *kind words that heal* be spoken about us in this life. And that those words will continue to *heal* long after we're gone.

> "A few days later, Jesus went out to a mountain to pray. He stayed there all night praying to God" (Luke 6:12).

(LP) Prayer Moves the Molecules of God's Heart

Boy, what must that feel like? I get ten to fifteen minutes in, and I'm either asleep, daydreaming, or I just run out of things to say—that's a personal confession, so you don't think you're the only one! But it may not be the length of time spent but the quality of it. Sometimes I feel more in tune when I just have a little short prayer and praise burst throughout the day. It's like being in a constant meditative state!

I find that positions have a lot to do with prayer time. If I'm horizontal, sleep is close behind; but if I'm vertical, or even walking while I pray, I feel more engaged. We each need to find what works for us because it's really more about our communication with our Heavenly Father than anything. He just wants to hear from us just like we check in with the wife or husband throughout the day—it's just a common courtesy for someone we love.

It's said in scripture, and I'm paraphrasing, that "He knows what we need before we ask Him." The benefits of connecting with our Savior in a heartfelt way has nothing but upside to it. Like praying over leftover food, it was already prayed over but praying again gives us another chance to love on our Father and thank Him for today's provisions. When we have an attitude like that, the *molecules of His heart* can't help but be affected. I know this to be true because when my children just call or text me for no reason, I feel all warm and fuzzy inside. It must be *molecules in my heart* moving!

I remember a time when we had a major fall off in our business. It took a big bite out of our income, so much so that we sincerely began to pray that our "God would supply all of our other needs, according to His riches in glory in Christ Jesus!" And I'm sure this sounds familiar, but we were in desperate prayer mode that day.

Like out of a Hollywood film, the doorbell rings. We looked at each other and said, "I hope that's not the guy coming to turn off our lights!" So I slowly walked toward the window to see if I saw a truck or a utility person. But when I peered through the window, no one was there, not even our normal neighborhood religious group.

When I opened the door, there was a FedEx envelope on the door mat. I hadn't ordered anything and wasn't expecting any overnight correspondence from anyone. Even the outside of the envelope didn't give any indication of where it was from. So I ripped off the strip and opened it. And as I reached in, there was a letter with a check in it! It was a payment from a group I had worked with, with no explanation as to why they were sending me a bonus! It was exactly the amount what we had hoped to receive, but the fact that it would come right at the time while we were praying was a shock! When we pray, *molecules of God's heart* get affected. And even more shocking than that, He knows exactly what we need before we ask Him!

"His ears are always open to our prayers." And prayer is *hidden treasures in your field*.

Verses 17–26 are the Beatitudes, which should be quoted in times of uncertainty, of which this life promotes a lot of. It's like what Jesus did in the desert when the enemy kept bombarding Him with negative options. We have to put our foot down like Jesus does on the enemy's neck and quote these Beatitudes as the outcome of those who are the blessed—a real jewel out of your *hidden treasures*.

But I say to you people who are listening to me, love your enemies. Ask God to bless the people who ask for bad things to happen to you. Pray for the people who are mean to you. If someone hits you on the side of your face, let them hit the other side too. If someone takes your coat, don't stop them from taking your shirt too. Give to everyone who asks you for something. When someone takes something that is yours, don't ask for it back. Do for others what you want them to do for you. (Luke 6:27–31)

(LP) Love Is Always a Good Response

"Do for others what you want them to do for you" (Luke 6:31).

This has got to be the most challenging of all God's words. I don't know about you, but love is not my first thought when I feel wronged in some way. However, as followers of Christ, even if we feel taken advantage of, our *responses* should always be Christlike.

I remember in the beginning of my walk, I really felt like a narcissist. Everything was centered around me, but now the whole world seems to suffer from that same affliction, as they see how many followers they can get on social media. Jesus nailed it with the words, and I paraphrase, "In the last days, people will be lovers of self," and come to find it was prophetic because selfies are the craze of our time.

I agree that the world is changing, and this scripture sounds a little old fashion in this context. But think about this, there have been a lot of movements that seemed like the hot thing at the time. But guess what's still lasting through the years? The Gospel. For a teaching to last these many thousands of years is honorable. And as God continues to encourage us to treat each other with *love*, I believe that too will carry through the years.

I'm always reminded of that when it comes to material things. We never see a U-Haul hooked up to the back of a hearse, right?

But, of course, I did hear the story about a guy who wanted to have all his money buried with him. He told his wife, "When I die, I want you to put all of my money into the casket with me." She was really upset at his request because it meant that he didn't care about what happened to her after he was no longer there to provide. Obviously, *love* was the furthest thing from his heart.

But the day came, and he passed away. The wife's girlfriend, who knew all about the husband's request, asked her if she had put all his money with him in the casket. And she told her friend, "Yep, that's exactly what I did…I wrote him a check!"

> If you love only those who love you, should you get any special praise for doing that? No, even sinners love those who love them! If you do good only to those who do good to you, should you get any special praise for doing that? No, even sinners do that! If you lend things to people, always expecting to get something back, should you get any special praise for that? No, even sinners lend to other sinners so that they can get back the same amount!
>
> I'm telling you to love your enemies and do good to them. Lend to people without expecting to get anything back. If you do this, you will have a great reward. You will be children of the Most High God. Yes, because God is good even to the people who are full of sin and not thankful. Give love and mercy the same as your Father gives love and mercy. (Luke 6:32–36)

(LP) Love's Prayer

If we can play by these rules, everything gets put into sync.

Oh God, we pray for this to become a reality—that it will be spoken from the president, to the Congress, CEO's, Fortune 500 companies, dignitaries, foreigners, and special interest groups, to everyday lay people, children, and the elderly. Make this our *mantra*: to love everyone, expecting nothing in return. Even those we don't favor that much, may our love continue toward different ethnicities, different beliefs, different religions, different class of people and sexual orientation! We have been commanded to *love everyone*. We can at least get that one right for the sake of our Lord. This is *love's prayer*, a *hidden treasure in your field*.

> "Do for others, what you want them to do for you. Give to others, and you will receive. You will be given much. It will be poured into your hands—more than you can hold. You will be given so much that it will spill into your lap. The way you give to others is the way God will give to you" (Luke 6:31, 38).

(LP) Blessings Are Chasing after You!

When I do concerts—the music presentation, the message, the altar call, and the marriage vows—I do them as if I were sitting out in the audience and trying to get valuable information from this person—words and music that will confirm and reconfirm the road God has called many to and remembering *the way you give to others is the way God will give to you.*

I say this very humbly, if there is such a thing, with what I'm going to share. For many years if there was someone that I was close to that didn't have transportation, I would find a way to hook them up. Now that I've been working with Findlay Toyota and now with Subaru of Las Vegas, I seem to be setting up deals for my friends. If I'm driving a reliable car, I want them to have one too. That's the translation of this scripture.

In concerts, I generally take a youngster from the audience and have them run after me up and down the aisle and up and down the stairs. The purpose of the exercise is to show my fans that when you give, *blessings chase after you*. I even stop abruptly and my young friend generally slams into my back to illustrate that not only do blessing run after us when we give, but they also overtake us.

Be encouraged today in the fact that you don't have to give a huge gift, like a car, to get blessed—just as long as your heart is in the right place when you give. Case in point, Jesus talked about a lady in the scriptures who only had two pennies to give but because she gave from the heart in a selfless sort of way in the eyes of our Lord, she gave more than the wealthy. To give creates more *hidden treasures in your field.*

> "Good people have good things saved in their hearts. That's why they say good things. But those who are evil have hearts full of evil, and that's why they say things that are evil. What people say with their mouths comes from what fills their hearts" (Luke 6:45).

(LP) What Fills Your Heart, Fills Your Mouth!

In self-evaluation, we should all take notice of what is creeping its way into our hearts. If we are seeing a significant change in our language, especially if cursing has become the norm of the day, we have to ask ourselves, is the heart being filled with negativity and agitation or words of peace and comfort? It all tells *what fills the heart.*

I say this to my shame, but I remember a time in the beginning of my ministry when I would watch some questionable comedians. I thought I was so spiritual that nothing could affect me, even foul language.

One night in particular, I had just finished a concert and was still hyped from all the previous activity. I decided to turn on the TV and watch a very popular comedian. He was an African American who was having his first HBO special. Out of curiosity, I watched. Again, his approach to comedy had very funny aspects to it. But I wondered why he had to use so much profanity to make a point. Well, I couldn't listen to all of it because of the language, so I turned it off.

One of our sons was just a baby then, so I had kept the sound down so he wouldn't wake up. But he woke up anyway, just like he did most nights. His little voice seemed to be extra irritating, especially since I had just finally fallen asleep.

The next thing I knew I sat up in the bed and yelled at the top of my lungs some harsh words, followed by profanity! Of course, it woke up the other family members who were shocked at my outburst. They had never heard me say words like that before, and honestly, it scared me too, so much so that I thought I might have just given back my salvation.

Watching the comedian's performance that evening opened a door for unexcusable words to creep into my heart. And even though that was thirty-five years ago, I am still embarrassed today at my outburst. It taught me that the things we entertain from the dark side can creep its way into our hearts without us even knowing it.

So what is the solution or antidote for this sort of behavior? Well, I believe that everything in our lives has a root. This attitude could have developed at an early stage in life and has been secretly growing centimeter by centimeter through the years.

My suggestion would be to go to our Father in true sincerity and repent. Ask Him if He could help show you the root that has continually caused you to have a heart-and-mouth disease. Identify it for what it is, an evil influence. And like the Bible says about the wheat and the weeds growing together, we've got to get out the spiritual weed cutter and start whacking away!

As you pray for renewal in your specific areas of fallacy, separate it and unravel it from your beautiful heart. It may be painful at first because it has become so interwoven that it can appear as something you need to keep for emotional and defensive reasons when in actuality it has been the cancer that has been choking out your God sensitivity and replacing it with abnormal reactions.

As God starts this excavation, starting at the root, you will recognize the change when your language starts changing. Even when you've yanked a lot of the weeds out, there may be a few lying over by the side of the road, whispering to you to resurrect them again. They know they're dying and they know by manipulating you they can continue to live.

But when you hear their voices, turn up the spiritual music and "sing unto the Lord, a new song, for He loves to hear our praises. Let all of creation sing, glory to our God, bow down before Him. Halleluiah, Glory to God. Halleluiah, Glory to God!" And guess what? Even when you stop singing, the outside interference will have lost it power and influence over you for a season.

Like a rudder that can steer a huge ship, the tongue can have a positive or negative effect on the course of our lives. And if mouth disease starts to come back, get out the spiritual mouthwash of prayer and praise.

Your heart will grow stronger in time. The most sensitive time is after your weed operation.

"Let the words of my mouth and the meditation of my heart, be acceptable in thy sight...oh Lord, you are my strength and my redeemer." Your close friends and family will be the first to give ya a high five for the new you!

Now get back out there and date, you single people. Let's try this new you out. Also, don't be afraid to entertain new business opportunities. Keep remembering that you are a work in progress. Find books, music, civil entertainment that will help maintain this new level of awareness, and you will find yourself on a new road with new opportunities. Thank God for a renewed heart, and continue filling it with words of deliverance and thanksgiving because He is the only one that can "create in us a clean heart and renew a right spirit with us." Thank you, Lord, for this helpful *hidden treasure*. The lesson continues...

> The people who come to me, who listen to my teachings and obey them—I will show you what they are like: They are like a man building a house. He digs deep and builds his house on rock. The floods come, and the water crashes against the house. But the flood cannot move the house, because it was built well.
>
> "But the people who hear my words and do not obey are like a man who builds a house with-

out preparing a foundation. When the floods come, the house falls down easily and is completely destroyed." (Luke 6:47–49)

(LP) A Sure Foundation

Wow, what an admonishment! The key to this dialogue is *foundation*. We should have a foundation under every aspect of our lives—in romance, in finance, in our spiritual life, and in our social life. If the foundation is firm, no matter what is said or done to us, we won't be shook. I mention shook because I'm from San Francisco, where a strong foundation can truly make a huge difference. That city can shake you without any warning.

There is a scripture in 1 Samuel 2:8 that says, "He raises the poor from the dust and lifts the needy from the ash heap; he seats them with princes and has them inherit a throne of honor. For the foundations of the earth are the Lord's; on them he has set the world."

This is an important word because I see the Bible that way. It is the base from which everything should stem. Many may disagree on certain passages because they may want to engage in an opposing lifestyle. But if we as humans are to find our footing again, there needs to be a standard that we all agree is *the* standard and we should base our moves off that.

All I know from my short time on this planet is, whenever I have wandered off the path from following his *foundation* plan for my life, I always pay the price for my deviation. Most times the Lord doesn't punish me to the degree I desire, but then the guilt trip sets in, and I am so sorry that I let my precious Lord down again.

I wrote a song years ago, inspired by a trip to the Holy Land. The passage was taken from, Isaiah 28:16, "I lay in Zion, for a foundation a stone, a tried stone a precious cornerstone a sure foundation, he that believeth shall not make haste." The ERV says it this way, "See, I lay a stone in Zion, a tested stone, a precious cornerstone for a sure foundation; the one who relies on it will never be stricken with panic."

In 1989 there was a devastating earthquake in San Francisco. It was around 6.9 to 7 magnitude. I was living in Glendale, California, at the time; and I was out at my favorite restaurant in the Beverly Hills area when I heard the news. My Mama Doll's house was not far from the Golden Gate Park and my sister Patsy was working downtown on the thirtieth floor. Of course, I was in panic when I heard the news but couldn't get through to anyone because the phone lines were jammed.

As I kept trying, I finally got through to my aunt Edith—my mom's sister, whose husband helped me build my studio in Oakland—just as Mama Doll and Patsy were coming through the door, checking on her. What a relief that was!

As I heard the story later, my sister's building swayed but did not have any substantial damage. In fact, she walked down the stairs with the other employees and did something I had never heard of her doing before. She walked all the way home from downtown San Francisco to Mama Doll's house in the famed Haight-Ashbury district!

As Patsy is telling me the story, she recalled not even being aware of going up and downhill in semi-high-heeled shoes. She said all her thoughts were geared on the safety of Mama Doll. When she arrived at the house, which was a two-story Victorian-style home, all the granite steps were cracked right down the middle. When she came into the house and saw only minor damage and Mama sweeping up debris, she just broke down and cried in relief.

Experts said that had they not been prepared with retrofits of buildings and such it could have been utterly devastating. I admit that life sometimes has some Jell-O in it, but the more we prepare, the less damage we'll have in a life quake. *Retrofit* is a neat word to remember. As we prepare our life's infrastructure daily, having a firm *foundation* under every aspect of our lives is the key—and a valuable *hidden treasure*.

Luke 7

You need only to give the order, and my servant will be healed. I know this because I am a man under the authority of other men. And I have soldiers under my authority. I tell one soldier, "Go," and he goes. And I tell another soldier, "Come," and he comes. And I say to my servant, "Do this," and my servant obeys me.

—Luke 7:7–8

(LP) Pray *Absolute* Prayers

This is the *absolute* of Jesus's authority, and if we believe it without a doubt, it will project us into a realm of faith that cannot be shaken—unless you live in San Francisco, of course! He came to seek and to save those who were lost. He is the Alpha and the Omega, the beginning and the end. He created the world. In Him all things hold together. His blood that He shed on Calvary washes away all our sins. *Absolutes*—our prayers and intercession should be absolute prayers!

When praying for people, don't pray *if* prayers. Make it a positive prayer for them, something for them to aspire to and reach toward.

I did a concert in Wentzville, Missouri, and a fan came up to me at the album table after the concert and announced that she needed a car. My prayer must have worked because my next trip through, she couldn't wait to get to the album table to tell me the good news. To my point, I do remember being specific, except for the color. If I was really on my game, I should have prayed for her favorite color too—like the scripture below.

"When Jesus heard this, he was amazed. He turned to the people following him and said, 'I tell you, this is the most faith I have seen anywhere, even in Israel'" (Luke 7:9).

(LP) Faith *Is* an Action Word!

Even Jesus was amazed at this kind of faith. We should believe in Him so much that He is touched by our non-wavering faith and tenacity! He did command us to ask, seek, and knock—all three denote persistence mixed with patience. It's a powerful combination and gets us ready for any battle in our lives. "Faith is the assurance of things hoped for, the evidence of things, not seen." *Faith is an action word!*

I remember a time specifically when my faith was much needed. I had just transitioned from Santana to Hosanna, and I needed an electronic keyboard for my concerts. In those days, the Yamaha CP 70 was the newest most innovative of its time. It was a miniature-looking baby grand and the hottest thing on the market. My prayer to God was that someone would donate it to my ministry. So I went right to the source—the Yamaha plant itself in Southern California. When I got through telling them what I had just done, leaving Santana and all and my new call to the lost, they looked at me like I had a third eye! I thought it was a very good plea, but they didn't waste any time saying *no* and then laughed me out of the building! Of course, I was devastated but when my *faith* kicked in, I realized that they were not the only game in town. The way I looked at it was, maybe God wanted to bless someone else back for giving me that gift.

I called around many places between San Francisco and Los Angeles. I met with most of the shops that were carrying the piano. As I got more committed to my prayer life, I could feel my faith growing with every appeal but no one saw the vision—until I got to the last place on my list. It was a small music store near San Jose.

During all these weeks of searching, I continued doing concerts and noticed that the offerings were increasing by a few dollars here and there and I had accumulated an additional $1,500 dollars! My first thought was that somebody in the family was going to get sick and would need this overage, or their fridge was going to go out.

When I spoke with the owner of the music store, he listened very intently to my plea, and toward the end of our talk, he told me that he too shared the same faith and belief in God. And with him saying that, I figured his next line would be, "So I decided to give you the piano!" Not really! Ha-ha. But he took a pause and said, "You know, this piano is the first of its kind and I'm already behind in orders even at $4,000 dollars a keyboard. But I tell you what, let me pray about it over the weekend and you call me on Monday and I'll have an answer for you." Wow! That was good! There is hope! I thanked him and gave him the biggest hug I could muster up. As you can imagine that was one of the longest weekends of my life. I fasted and prayed and hoped that there would be a favorable answer on Monday.

Well, when the beginning of the week came, I was like a little kid waiting to see what Santa left under the tree. So about 11:00 a.m. I made the call and the owner asked if I was far away. I told him I was right over the hill in Santa Cruz. He said, "Would you mind coming over?" I said, "Sure!" I was there in forty-five minutes.

When I walked into the store, my heart was beating out of my chest. It wasn't like my whole life depended on this instrument. But in my mind's eye, I could see the ministry possibilities, given that bands were really having a struggle in those days.

When we sat down to talk, his words to me were similar to ones I heard before. But he added one part I was surprised about, and it was this: He said, "I've gone over and over in my head how we could make this piano a blessing for you. But I keep coming up with the same scenario about the cost, but this is what I'm willing to do. It cost me 1,500 wholesale, and I would be willing to forgo my $2,500 profit on it, so you can have this piano for your ministry."

I didn't even have to think about it and stood up and said, "*Yes, yes, yes!*" Not only was he selling me something that retailed for $4,000, but the $1,500 was the exact amount I had accumulated! Needless to say, that piano has literally been with me all over the world, even as far as Israel on one occasion.

During the writing of this book, I was surprisingly contacted by the generous donor, Barry Wineroth. We caught up over the phone and said he has been watching my ministry progress since the eighties. We remain close friends.

As the book of James reminds us, when *faith* is put into *action*, it's literally unstoppable. When you think there is no way, "He makes a way out of no way." If we trust Him to do it, something always happens to our benefit, every time. *Faith mixed with action* is a *huge hidden treasure in your field.*

> Right then Jesus healed many people of their sicknesses and diseases. He healed those who had evil spirits and made many who were blind able to see again. Then he said to John's followers, "Go tell John what you have seen and heard: The blind can see. The crippled can walk. People with leprosy are healed. The deaf can hear. The dead are brought back to life. And the Good News is being told to the poor. Great blessings belong to those who don't have a problem accepting me." (Luke 7:21–23)

(LP) Stay Humble

Pastor Mel is from the St. Louis area, and I agree that when you're in a rural area of the world, more miracles seem to happen. It's because the people have nowhere else to turn. They are as desperate as the lady in the Bible with the issue of blood. In over-preached and over-saturated areas, people have options, opinions, and attitude. To a great degree their faith can be a little, like they've seen it all already!

I have a dear friend named Mario Murillo who is an evangelist and a healer. I asked him once, "How do you know when people are being touched and healed in your meetings." And he said, "God whispers the condition of the person in my ear, and right then, I know who they are." I was amazed at that answer. When people attend his gatherings, it can come off a little like the movie *Leap of Faith* with Steve Martin. But Mario's healings are authentic.

So I put it to the test myself. I said, "Lord, I want that ability too, to pray for hurting people that haven't been able to get cured by conventional means." Not long after I spoke it, it started to happen.

My next concert was in Denver, Colorado, at a convention center there. Again, as I was singing "We Must Believe," I saw a picture in my mind's eye of a small white light on one side of my forehead. Just to check and see if it were the lights or not, I opened my eyes and started looking around. I soon concluded that the lights that were shining on me were shaped different than the one I was seeing when I closed my eyes.

It was quite something to experience, but I knew instinctively that someone's eyes were being healed, so I called it out. And sure enough, a lady a few rows from the front stood up and said, "It's me. It's me!" And surprisingly enough, a few rows behind her, another person stood up with the same healing. Both came to the concert blind in one eye and walked out seeing in both.

In that instance I got a tiny, tiny glimpse of what our Lord experiences every time one of his children receive such an overwhelming blessing. But to my shame, I started thinking I was a big part of why this phenomenon was occurring. After a few short years of these wonderful visitations from our Lord, it faded as fast as it came. These type of healings on a continual basis have to be submerged in *humility*. It's not something just for show.

I have since repented and taking a more humble approach to this serious call. And again, He has allowed the supernatural to accompany my prayers. The scripture promises, "Humble thyself in the sight of the Lord, and He will lift you up." This doesn't mean that your voice has to be all soft but definitely your heart does. A *hidden treasure* for us evangelist to remember!

"Listen! I will send my messenger ahead of you.
He will prepare the way for you" (Luke 7:27).

(LP) God Always Prepares the Way

The Lord is using today's technology for His purpose. Pastors and lay people are telling their friends on TV, Facebook, YouTube, Instagram, e-mails, Twitter, and every other technology. It's a new means of *preparing the way*.

I had a season in the late eighties when I went through a burnout. It was the staff from the Jack Hayford Ministries that God *prepared* ahead of time to walk me through it. They not only pulled me out of my quicksand but were patient enough to wash my stinking self off. It was a painful and embarrassing experience in that many that had looked to me as a really Jesus representative were starting to doubt our Lord because of what I was going through. In all honesty, I tried to wear the face and the façade, but the real me kept bleeding through. I even got a scripture about "Foreigners, rebuilding my walls." And finally, in the early nineties, that happened.

The suggestion from Pastor Jack's ministry was that I stop doing concerts for a while. I knew I had to do it, but panic swept over me in that, how was I going to maintain my livelihood for what looked to me like a long season of time. So I immediately put my house on the market, along with all of my brand-new recording equipment. I even had some kickback from my hairdresser about selling my recording studios. But he didn't know how serious I was about a change.

There were many people across the country praying for God's restoration in my life. And they told me so by correspondence. But again, I wasn't use to sitting on the sidelines and watching what I thought were golden years and opportunities pass me by.

The whole process took two years! During this time, I was getting words of encouragement from scriptures and prayer that God was preparing opportunities for me that had not occurred in my previous life, even a very specific word about "Foreigners rebuilding my walls!"

After my two-year sabbatical, I got released by the Hayford camp, following a men's weekend retreat. I remember it like it was yesterday. Pouring out my heart to the Lord all day every day caused me to create unbelievable songs of deliverance. I didn't think about them becoming a part of an album at the time, I just needed a way to convey to our Lord my true emotions. The gift He gave me, when applied sincerely, always touches the heart of our Savior. But when I sang one of them at the retreat, it was a cue to the Hayford camp that it was time to release me back into ministry.

I couldn't wait to get back on the road and test out my new spiritual legs. My first outreach was to Russia and the Ukraine. It was truly "foreigners rebuilding my walls" and my compassion for people again.

The average person over there is nothing like the negatives we keep hearing concerning their leaders. In fact, the people are the exact opposite. They are the most gentle and loving human beings I have ever met.

For instance, when my engineer Vince and I would walk on Christiac Street in Kiev, people would walk up to us and just start a conversation. Many could barely speak English, but with sign language and facial expressions, we were able to communicate just fine. And even though most of them were just common folk and not wealthy by any means, they would search through there belonging to give us a gift before we parted ways. Most of our gifts were pencils or a ruble, which equaled two cents. How precious! God not only had this great country embrace me so warmly, but my engineer Vince Sanchez met his bride in Kiev. That's a whole other wonderful story in itself. Maybe he will elaborate in his book! Suffice to say he is still married to her, starting in the early nineties and have a beautiful, talented, and intellectual daughter.

Then as I mentioned before, meeting my little Filipino woman on the cruise was another fulfillment of God's promise to "rebuild my walls."

God continues until today, like He does in all our lives, to have someone up ahead of us, "holding up a flare." God's word is one of those flares. It's truly a "lamp to our feet and a light to our path." His preparatory person is a precious, precious *hidden treasure*, and I thank the Lord for having the insight to send much needed messengers ahead of me. My prayer for you, my friend, is to know that if he did it for me, he will do it for you! Don't give up on yourself. *God always prepares the way. A hidden treasure in your field.*

> "John the Baptizer came and did not eat the usual food or drink wine. And you say, 'He has a demon inside him.' The Son of Man came eating and drinking. And you say, 'Look at him! He eats too much and drinks too much wine! He is a friend of tax collectors and other sinners!' But wisdom is shown to be right by those who accept it" (Luke 7:33–35).

(LP) Truth Brings Relationships Closer

The reference to wine in the above scripture shows it was not grape juice as some interpret. It does not give a license to be drunk and unruly, but it references wine in a good light of which we as Christians don't hear about much. Not many want to address this from the pulpit because it is a controversial subject. But me, I have no worries about stirring up some stuff. If we could be more honest and up front about these types of likes and dislikes without judging each other, we would be way on down the road toward a more honest and *truthful* relationship.

I was at breakfast with a dear pastor friend of mine, and he ordered at least six cups of strong coffee. And to my surprise, he blurted out that it was the only legal high left. I so appreciated his honesty, and it gave me hope that if the truth thing is going to sweep through the nation, it's got to start with us.

We all must find piece with God in whatever we put in our body. It is the temple of the Holy Spirit, and there are many areas we can challenge ourselves on toward new levels concerning eating, drinking, coffee, soda, stress, positive mind-set, and even drinking water. In fact, I've got a *hidden treasure* to pass on to you. Check on www.leonslivingwater.com, you'll be shocked at what you will discover!

Researchers at the University of Notre Dame found most Americans lie about eleven times a week. They studied a group of 110 people from age 18 to 71 and asked half the group to reduce their lying over a ten-week period. Those participants who stopped lying—exaggerating their accomplishments, making false excuses for being late, and evading uncomfortable questions—had a significant improvement in their health and their social interactions.

That's why I feel this revival we keep waiting for is going to start with the youth. They haven't become so opinionated yet. They have enough God-given innocence in them that they believe every word that comes from the Savior's lips, like "Nothing is impossible for our Lord." They have just come from heaven and still have the smell of angels' wings.

In this time zone in history, the entertainment world is really capitalizing on truth programming, like reality TV, a genre of programming in which the everyday routines of "real life" people (as opposed to fictional characters played by actors) are followed closely by the cameras. In this genre, there are at least four major categories of shows: game shows, dating shows, talent shows, and plain follow-me-where-ever-I-go shows. The scope of reality television has increased steadily over the last couple of years, with shows like the *Kardashian*'s and the *Bachelor* gaining millions of views. Even the movie industry is capitalizing on this phenomenon by making movies based on "real life events."

"I think lying can cause a lot of stress for people, contributing to anxiety and even depression," Dr. Bryan Bruno, acting chairman of the department of psychiatry at Lenox Hill Hospital in New York City, told *Health Day*. "Lying less is not only good for your relationships, but for yourself as an individual. People might recognize the more devastating impact lying can have on relationships, but probably don't recognize the extent to which it can cause a lot of internal stress."

There is a thirst in mankind for truth, and being open and honest creates a bond of trust. The scriptures declare that "the truth will set you free."

I pray that we will push for more truth in our life, especially when it's uncomfortable and unpopular. Stand out in the world by shining brighter than the norm. Become like the shoreline that the water depends on to be there, to show where the boundaries are. Yes, it's a challenge, even by us God-fearing people. But one day at a time, we can be way on down the street in no time at all. The truth is one of our most powerful *hidden treasures in the field.*

> "I tell you that her many sins are forgiven. This is clear, because she showed great love. People who are forgiven only a little will love only a little" (Luke 7:47).

(LP) Forgiven More Than I Deserve

Our Lord has gone through such a horrible ordeal for us. It wasn't even His fault—the pain and anguish He had to endure on our behalf. That should be motivation enough to love much. Even though I have been forgiven for much less than some real tragic stories I have heard.

In 2011 Patricia Machin lost her husband when he set out to buy the morning paper. Gerrard Machin was doing what he always did, but this time would not return home. Patricia sensed something was wrong and went to look for him. She was greeted by the sight of an ambulance and blood on the ground. Her husband had been struck down by a driver.

The driver, Brian Williamson, was extremely distressed over having hit Gerrard Machin. Patricia Machin, though, felt no anger toward the driver. She knew that the horrible accident had not been intentional, and she harbored no ill will toward Williamson. The sincerity of her forgiveness shone through in a letter she wrote to Williamson that was to be used in his defense. In that letter she wrote, "However bad it was for me, I realize it was one thousand times worse for you." *Forgiven more than I deserve.*

On October 2, 2006, Charles C. Roberts walked into an Amish schoolhouse armed with three guns. There were twenty-six students in the schoolhouse. He allowed fifteen boys, a pregnant female student, and three other adult females with infant children to leave safely but held the remaining fifteen girls captive and tied their feet together.

His deranged rationale for his actions was that he wanted to exact revenge for something that had happened in his past. Notes that he left behind indicate anger toward himself and God for the death of his newborn daughter almost nine years earlier.

Authorities were alerted and soon arrived on the scene. Not long after police arrived, Roberts started shooting, killing three children and himself. Two more children died later from their injuries.

In the face of such tragedy, one can only imagine the hurt and anger the loved ones of the victims might feel. In an extraordinary demonstration of forgiveness, members of the Amish community, including family members of the deceased victims, attended Robert's funeral and comforted his widow. The Amish community did not stop there. They also offered financial support to Robert's widow. *Forgiven more than I deserve.*

Multiply that human forgives times infinity and that is only the beginning of God's forgiveness toward us!

Oh God, I do acknowledge my shortcomings today and throw myself at your feet. You have been and continue to be the greatest love gift I have ever received in my life. Some are in anticipation of a lottery win. Well, when I met you, that was a lotto win, without the possibility of spending it all up. And the times, Lord, when you seem to overlook the punishment stage of my sins, I know there must be a reason behind it all to not put on me more than I can bear. Amen!

As I look back over my life, I can see our Lord's fingerprints all over the place. If there had been DNA testing fifty years ago, Jesus would have been identified as a person of interest. Most of us don't want people all up in our business. But want to or not, I'm glad the Lord took the intuitive to be proactive concerning me. Martha Stewart and I suffered the same fate by making almost the same bad financial choices. One thing the experience taught me was that no matter how low we go, Jesus will get down on His knees to pull us up out of the gutter. I can say for myself that I am *forgiven more than I deserve.* And it is another *hidden treasure in the field.*

Luke 8

The next day, Jesus traveled through some cities and small towns. Jesus told the people a message from God, the Good News about God's kingdom.

—Luke 8:1

(LP) Full Package Delivery to Small Groups

It's good to know that Jesus the Christ went to small towns too and delivered the Good News about God's kingdom. So when my flesh starts to make ministry comparisons, I keep reminding myself that the author of life had no pride about making a *full package delivery to small groups*. Even Martin Luther King Jr. taught a philosophy course at college and had only six students in his class.

I remember a time not long ago when I decided to do a concert at a little church in Henderson, Nevada. I wasn't sure how many people would come, but we did pray beforehand that it would be a life-changing moment for everyone in attendance. I've got to tell you, not only was the Spirit of God thick in that place but the pastor gave us a book written by Wayne Cordeiro that continues to affect my life today. Little did I know that the book would put me on roads that I hadn't traveled down before—literally.

A short time after that, I was asked to sing at a publishers' Christmas event and my good friend and mentor Jack Hayford was in attendance because he was also a writer for this publishing group. And with all I had been through with Pastor John Wold and staff, it was good for him to see the new fruit of his labor.

After I got through with my performance, they invited a young man to the stage who also had a book published by the host company. He was very eloquent, well-educated, and very funny. He was from Hawaii, and every once in a while, he would break out in a broken, island-style English, which added to the already amusing way he had of presenting the Gospel.

After he was through, I congratulated him on such a rousing speech. He smiled and went on to tell me what my music had meant to him over the years. I was really blown away that he even knew me. He went on to ask me if I would be willing to come to his church in Hawaii. "Of course!" I said, not knowing if he could afford flying us over and such. Then he gave me his card, and you'll never guess what his name was. Yep, it was Wayne Cordeiro, the author of the book that had brought me such encouragement. When I told Pastor Jack about the invitation, he told me that I would really like the aloha spirit and the hearts of the people. Plus, he had a congregation of twelve thousand members!

I got on the horn the next day with Pastor Wayne and set everything in motion. But I asked him to keep it a secret because I wanted to surprise my wife on her birthday. So when the day came to leave, I told my wife that I was taking her on a surprise fortieth outing for her birthday. I told her we were flying somewhere and to bring an overnight bag.

When we got to the Orange County Airport, we took a flight to San Jose, California. I'm sure Renee was thinking, *What's up here that constitutes a fortieth birthday?* Then we walked over to another gate that said "Honolulu, Hawaii."

She asked, "Are we going to Hawaii, sweetheart?"

I said, "Yep!"

Then she said, "But I don't have any clothes."

I laughed and told her that I had brought her clothes over earlier, and they were underneath the plane, the lingerie too. Needless to say, it was a fortieth to remember.

The smile on her face when we landed was priceless, especially being a Filipino girl. It brought back all the smells, humidity, and warm breezes she had been missing.

This exciting adventure all started from a *full package delivery to a small group*. The lesson is to never despise anything small. Small groups, small beginnings, even small people. We have to remember this, even when a lot of people don't show up for our event, "it's not the quantity of the people but the quality."

Update: As we speak, we will be starting next year's worldwide tour in Hawaii. We have been there off and on now for a period of sixteen years. When opportunity knocks on your door, for something smaller than normal, it could be the nucleus of a much greater thing. But even if it doesn't, every life we have the privilege to touch and inspire is valuable. And realize that our God may have a *big* thing in store for another generation in a different time zone. This is not only a life lesson but a true *hidden treasure*.

> "No one lights a lamp and then covers it with a bowl or hides it under a bed. Instead, they put the lamp on a lamp stand so that the people who come in will have enough light to see" (Luke 8:16).

(LP) Light It Up

This phrase challenges me again, to take what I have produced and put it as high on the hill as I can so the whole world can see it: US, Europe, Japan. China, Africa, Korea, Brazil, Iraq, Iran, Afghanistan, Muslim countries, Jews, Mexicans, Filipinos, Australians, Indians— all nations. "Ask me for the nations and I will give them to you as your inheritance. The earth as your possession" (paraphrased).

It's in those *hidden treasures* that our uniqueness presents itself. The special way that we are and our contribution to our environment, God puts the puzzle pieces together so everyone has a part to play. And we should be thankful because He knows what the top of the puzzle box looks like and where each piece should fit.

At the writing of this book, my son Gabriel, or GabReal as he's calling himself, has the number one song in the country on the CCM Billboard charts called "Eye of the Storm." When I was helping him find the melody lines as a youngster, I hoped that one day he would carry on the legacy, especially during a time when only 4 percent of millennials are going to church. Our *light* should be on full even if we only have a forty-watt personality.

I say this because we have a Filipino friend name Emmie. She is a painter of paintings by craft and possess a sweet and gentle spirit. Emmie has been praying for her husband Roland to make a commitment to Christ. But every time she or anyone else would try and encourage him that way, he would blurt out, "I can't be Born Again because I'm Born Against!" It was sort of comical the way he would say it, but that was pretty much how he felt about religion. Emmie might be a quiet person, but when she would pray for her husband, she would take that forty-watt personality and *light it up!* So much so that a lot of us believed along with her that Roland would make a commitment of faith.

One day when we were having fellowship together over at Miss Marty's house, who is another dear person and friend, the subject came up about what we'd say to Jesus when asked what did we do with the life He gave us. It must have resonated with Roland because I turned and asked him in that moment, "Do you want to make sure that you are born again and not born against?" And to my surprise, he agreed to make a confession of faith to our Savior. So right there in Miss Marty's kitchen, with tears running down all our faces, we all held hands and prayed a prayer of salvation along with Roland. It was the happiest day of Emmie's life to experience her forty-watt prayers, making such an eternal impact on her husband. It was a good thing that it happened at that time because six months later he contracted an illness that attacked him pretty aggressively—and then he was gone.

I learned a valuable lesson through that experience. Never take any opportunity for granted and always keep your light shining, no matter what the watt. Reminds me of that song we use to sing in Sunday school:

"This little light of mine…I'm gonna let it shine.
This little light of mine…I'm gonna let it shine.
This little light of mine…I'm gonna let it shine.
Let it shine, let it shine, let it shine!"

"What kind of man is this? He commands the wind
and the water, and they obey him" (Luke 8:25).

(LP) Command It and It's Done

Clear the road in front of us, Oh God, concerning any distraction that would try and rob us from our appointed opportunities. Sometimes we have to imitate your Son and *command the wind and the water to obey us*! May our prayers be like the clouds in the sky, raining down exactly what each one needs, especially those that are called by your name, those that have been anticipating the unfolding of your promise to them.

When God commands a thing to be done for us, it's a done deal! For an example, Elijah listened to God's voice and God himself listened to Elijah. Their relationship was one that in the Old Testament was only reserved for priests and prophets.

> "Then he stretched himself upon the child three
> times and cried to the Lord, 'O Lord my God,
> let this child's life come into him again.' And the
> Lord listened to the voice of Elijah. And the life
> of the child came into him again. And he revived"
> (1 Kings 17:21–22).

These are God's words that are sitting in scripture waiting for us to implement!

John 15:7, "Stay joined together with me, and follow my teachings. If you do this, you can ask for anything you want, and it will be given to you."

Matthew 7:7, "Continue to ask, and God will give to you. Continue to search, and you will find. Continue to knock, and the door will open for you."

Jeremiah 33:3, "Pray to me, and I will answer you. I will tell you important secrets. You have never heard these things before."

Isaiah 65:24, "And it shall come to pass, that before they call, I will answer; and while they are yet speaking, I will hear."

Psalms 37:4, "Delight thyself also in the LORD; and he shall give thee the desires of thine heart."

John 16:24, "But ask in my name, and you will receive. And you will have the fullest joy possible."

I have had the good fortune to use these words with great results. The thing about these words is that they have a built in power of their own, because they remain tied to the power source. John 15:7 is saying the same thing to us. If we stay plugged into the power source, the same will happen for us. There will be a constant essence of the Holy One, available at all times, exhibiting God's existence from time to time, a true *hidden treasure in our field.*

> The man answered, "Legion." (He said his name was "Legion")...Then the demons came out of the man and went into the pigs. The herd of pigs ran down the hill into the lake, and all were drowned.
>
> The men who were caring for the pigs ran away and told the story in the fields and in the town. People went out to see what had happened. They came to Jesus and found the man sitting there at the feet of Jesus. The man had clothes on and was in his right mind again; the demons were gone. This made the people afraid. The men who saw these things happen told the others all about how Jesus made the man well. (Luke 8:33–36)

(LP) This too Shall Pass

The line that got me was verse 35, "The *man had clothes on and was in his right mind again.*"

I have often wondered when people have a setback—like a doctor I heard about who got laid off from his job and decided to kill his four kids, his wife, then turned the gun on himself—the pressure must have seemed so enormous to them that they figured there is no other way out. And I say "they" because his wife was also in on the arrangement.

As we all know, we can hit a season in our lives where everything seems to fall apart. Like the Humpty Dumpty slogan that says, "All the king's horses and all the king's men couldn't put Humpty Dumpty back together again." Why? Because it's not the government's job, that's God's job. In all fairness God could use the government, but the ultimate credit should go to our Savior.

It's in times like these that we have to scratch beneath the surface and dig up a *hidden treasure*, like a past experience when God delivered us. There are undiscovered *treasures* that will be revealed right on time. Just keep telling yourself, "Just one more day…just one…more…day."

There was a season in my life when I thought I was going to be homeless. You are probably saying, "Leon Patillo, with all that talent he has! How could that even be possible?" Well, as the saying goes, "But for the grace of God, there go I."

It was during a time when I had put all my eggs in one basket. In the back of my mind, I knew I should have kept some other activities in play. You know how you get that feeling deep down in your gut when the Holy Spirit is trying to guide you, direct you, and even project a future event? Well, I didn't listen, and the next thing I knew, I was being let go from my job, and within months an eviction notice was put on my door. It's the first time in my Christian life that I really got scared! What would I tell my family? What could I possibly say to my many friends and fans? But one thing that it did do was it gave me a better understanding and sympathy for a person who would consider not waking up the next day. In times like these that we need to remember to say to ourselves, out loud, "*This too shall pass!*"

One valuable lesson I learned from my experience was that I knew God had a future and a hope for me. From the time God formed me in my mother's womb, I was predestined for a special call—and my particular journey didn't have defeat in its vocabulary. So as a result of a lot of prayer and searching out scriptures, the passage about "ask and it shall be given to you" came up in my spirit. I very prayerfully called my creditors, explained the situation, and worked out a repayment plan. And do you know that every single one of them were willing to work with me? This is another *hidden treasure* we should never forget.

In my cartoon mind, I see our Heavenly Father poking the angels in the side with his elbow saying, "Watch this." And I'm sure the ones who are standing near the Father are covering their ribs because as soon as the Father's prediction comes to pass for us, God pokes another angel in the ribs, saying "See, I told ya…I told ya!" So right now there are hundreds, maybe thousands, of sore-rib angels in heaven. And those angels are angels that just pertain to you. There have got to be thousands, even millions, of angels, backing away from the Father when something God has promised us comes to pass. "His word will never return void, without accomplishing what He sent it to do." That's a *treasure* that should be built into every day, especially in the low days. *Remember, this too shall pass. "The man had clothes on and was in his right mind again."*

> *"So Jesus got into the boat to go back to Galilee. The man he had healed begged to go with him. But Jesus sent him away, saying, 'Go back home and tell people what God did for you.' So the man went all over town telling what Jesus had done for him"* (Luke 8:37–39).

(LP) Go Tell Somebody

This is a good hint as to what we should do, every time something fantastic happens in our lives. *Go tell somebody!* Even though it may not seem like a big story to you, it could make a profound impact on someone else because you never know what they could be facing in their lives that day. Another thing to remember is that Jesus has a way of using us to touch a life, even when there is no expression coming from others. I know this to be true because of our concerts in Japan.

The fans in that part of the country not only enjoy the music, they listen to every word and musical note that's being presented. My experience has been that they never gave me a loud reaction while I was performing. But at the end of each song, they would begin to clap harder, louder and longer than most of my fans across the country. Then, at the closing song, you can look around the arena and see many of them crying because they know that we won't see each other again for many years.

I remember one occasion at a Presbyterian Church in Idaho when I was playing to a very conservative senior citizens' congregation. I played for them like I do every place with a rousing beginning mixed with words of faith and encouragement and a powerful heartfelt ending. During the service, they just watched me like a movie. But at the album table, many came up to me to say what a powerful, moving service it was! And each one continued to tell me the personal parallels between the songs, my message, and what they were going through! So you can't tell from an outward appearance what is going on for someone internally. Just tell folks about the *hidden treasures in your field* so they can find *treasures* in theirs!

> "While Jesus was going to Jairus' house, the people crowded all around him. A woman was there who had been bleeding for twelve years. She had spent all her money on doctors, but no doctor was able to heal her. The woman came behind Jesus and touched the bottom of his coat. At that moment, her bleeding stopped. Then Jesus said, 'Who touched me?'" (Luke 8:42–45).

(LP) No Power Shortage with God

The story above of the woman with the blood issue is evidence that your faith can be so strong that it pulls power from the Holy One. Also, if we have a sickness that the physician can't heal, Jesus has that capability—be it physical, mental, psychological, or habitual.

I have a good friend and pastor in Arcadia, California, named Pastor Tom Shriver. In this back nine of his life, he has finally found the mate that he has been praying for in Janie. A few years back I got the privilege of performing the wedding. It was a festive occasion that was well attended by family and friends that wanted to experience God's promise to Tom.

Well, about eighteen months ago, Janie was diagnosed with stage four cancer. And because of the doctor's prognosis, she immediately quit her job to get her affairs in order. As you can suspect, all of us were in desperate prayer for her, in hopes that she would last for at least another six months.

In the meantime, we thought maybe this new alkaline water we discovered could help her body to heal itself. Well, along with that and her medication, she has continued to live another three years.

I got a call from Pastor Tom last week with an incredible report. He told me that they had run some more test and discovered that her cancer was shrinking! We had all been praying, but you never know how God is going to answer sometimes because we know that the ultimate healing is to be in that new body that will never suffer pain or die again. But God has chosen to show us that there is *no power shortage* on this side of heaven as well!

Another testimony below:

> "Jesus said to her, 'My daughter, you are made well because you believed. Go in peace'" (Luke 8:48).

My lola, Renee's mother, is in her nineties and has been having health problems for the last four decades. One afternoon she was rushed to the hospital because of a mild heart attack. The family was with her around the clock. When one would leave, the next person would grab a chair and blanket and camp out. The prognosis looked bleak for her, and we all discussed the possibility of putting her into a hospice facility. But on this day of discussion, I really felt in my spirit that God had other plans. So we all held hands—me and Renee's faithful Catholic brothers and sisters—and I sent up a prayer of faith. Well, she lasted four more years after that prayer and is now back in the arms of her husband Leon, who left us fifteen years ago. There is *no power shortage with God!*

I learned a valuable lesson during that experience. When someone asks you to pray and you know what their heart's desire is, that's the prayer we should offer in faith. I know for a fact, if I was sick and someone came to pray for me, I would tell them what I would like the Lord to do for me and would expect a prayer along those lines, not an if-a, could-a, want-a, might-a kind of prayer but a real prayer of belief and affirmation.

I have heard it over and over again, from the medical field to the pulpit, that people usually reach toward the thing that you say to them. If you tell someone, for instance, that he's no good, he will have a tendency to reach toward that expectation. If you put the bar up high in your conversation, people have a tendency to reach for that outcome. Our words are so powerful that Jesus even called himself The Word.

Any goal that I'm trying to accomplish in my life, physically, mentally, emotionally, career-wise, or any other challenge, I want people rallying around me with faith, positive faith, realizing that if we put everything into His hands, there is *no power shortage with God!* That person becomes to me a *hidden treasure in my field,* as we continue below:

> Everyone was crying and feeling sad because the girl was dead. But Jesus said, "Don't cry. She is not dead. She is only sleeping."
>
> The people laughed at him, because they knew that the girl was dead. But Jesus held her hand and called to her, "Little girl, stand up!" Her spirit came back into her, and she stood up immediately. Jesus said, "Give her something to eat." The girl's parents were amazed. He told them not to tell anyone about what happened. (Luke 8:52–56)

(LP) What Some Folks See as Dead, Jesus Sees as Sleeping!

Joseph is still one of my favorite characters in the Bible. Any analogy that I can draw from him, I try to. In Joseph's case, after being sold into slavery and then ending up in jail, one would think, his dream of having the family bow down to him one day was way out of reach. *But what some see as dead, Jesus sees sleeping.* So I say to you today, my friend, don't judge yourself or others that you might be praying for as dead. God has skills, my friend. There is nothing impossible for our Lord. As Moses said when the enemy army was behind him and the Red Sea was in front of him, "Do not be afraid. Stand firm and you will see the deliverance the Lord will bring you today" (Exod. 14:13).

This is why I love the story of Lazarus because there was a physical death and resurrection that no one had ever seen up until that point, a physical dead body being brought out of a tomb, unwrapped, and started breathing and walking around. When we see this sort of thing today, it's normally in horror movies or a Michael Jackson video—but not in real life. Which, when God has His mind made up to perform a miracle, *His spiritual effects* are *way* more powerful than Hollywood!

In Lazarus's case, he had been dead for four days. Jesus could have awakened him before that time, according to his schedule and location. But the belief in those days was that the spirit of a person hovered over the body for a few days. And Jesus didn't want this miracle to get caught up in that superstition.

So realize in your analogies in life that *Jesus* truly *"is the resurrection and the life. He who believes in me, though he were dead, yet shall he live." What some folks see as dead, Jesus sees as sleeping!*

At this juncture, I thought I would insert a few verses from the beloved 1 Corinthians 13. I found some *hidden treasures* there that I thought might assist you on your love quest. If love permeates our being, life will spring from it. There is no chronological reason I'm doing this, I just thought it might provide another side of JC!

> "I may speak in different languages, whether human or even of angels. But if I don't have love, I am only a noisy bell or a ringing cymbal. I may have the gift of prophecy, I may understand all secrets and know everything there is to know, and I may have faith so great that I can move mountains. But even with all this, if I don't have love, I am nothing" (1 Cor. 13:1–2).

(LP) Love Can Conquer All

A lot of us mask our feelings in service so that when we are questioned about our motives we can point them toward the service we do. But the essence of love is like a nun in a chapel—no one knows her name but she has dedicated her life to pray and intercede for the world. If questioned, she has hit such a stride in her love that she may not even understand the question.

I got the blessing years ago to go to the Vatican in Rome. Even though I had seen pictures of it, to stand in front of this man-made marvel was only something you can experience in person. As I walked in the front door, there was a chapel on the right side where the nuns prayed. I must say I have done concerts for many denominations in my career, but I have never felt the presence of God so thick and peaceful as I did in that room.

I pray for this type of love expression in your life that doesn't need fanfare. Just simple jesters, like saying "God bless you," when someone sneezes. That's a big thing in an office of non-saved hearts. In my line of work, there is a lot of publicity surrounding my concerts, CDs, books, etc. So my actions really have to be put into check. You may have a job where your PR could make the difference concerning your success. But to be aware of that consciously will help us not succumb to the temptation of our publicity. Especially with social media, everybody is under pressure to show the world what is happening in their environments.

My new stepped-up outreach to the youth involve getting my *Ready 2 Rise* CD to as many youngsters as I can at no cost to them. And because of the division that seems to be sweeping through our land, we are also on a campaign to get my other CD, *Worship and Healing*, into the hands of their parents and grandparents.

To the point, who *I am* in Christ should always outweigh what *I do* for Him. A *hidden treasure* I am aspiring to every day.

"Love is patient..." (1 Cor. 13:4).

(LP) Listening Are the Legs Patience Stands On

Prayer and meditation are the key for patience. When we pray, it's letting God know how much we appreciate everything that he does for us, ask Him to forgive us for our shortcomings, and a time to make request for our needs. Then after this time of gratitude and personal expression, we meditate. Meditation is generally the time that we are quiet so we can hear His response to our prayer. In times of meditation, visions, dreams, and priorities become so clear that sometimes for me I hate to walk away to go do the thing.

That must be why monks can spend so much time in prayer and meditation. Even the famous scripture tells us, "They that wait upon the Lord, will renew their strength, they will mount up with wings as eagles. They will run and not be weary they will walk and not faint." It is a daily flesh training session that we should all strive to achieve. A definite *hidden tre*asure.

"It does not brag, and it is not proud" (1 Cor. 13:4).

(LP) A *True* Outward Expression of an Inner Conviction

There is a way to convey your exuberance and passion for our Savior. And a few saints of old give us that context, like King David for instance when he danced before the Lord. He was boasting in his God. When John the Baptist was loud, down at the lake, it was to bring attention to Israel's sins and pave a pathway for our Lord. So, in all fairness, we shouldn't misinterpret external exuberance for bragging or being proud in the worldly sense. It just happens to be the personality type of some people.

As a musical artist, there is always a fine line. But that line happens for many that have others looking on for guidance, like a coach, the boss, a teacher, even a mom and dad. We all have been given some measure of authority in our circles, but maintaining a humble heart is the perfect ingredient for a person of authority. Jesus had tremendous power and leverage over His followers, but those around Him were drawn to His human compassion; how He was so proactive toward lepers and the outcast; how he praised the sacrificial gifts of those who didn't have a lot to give, like the widow; and, the ultimate, of dying for the very people He created. That is *a true outer expression of an inner conviction*—and a pure *hidden treasure* for us to live by.

But the bottom line for us is to dip our gifts into the deep honey of humility and we will always come up tasting like our sweet Lord.

> "Love does not remember wrongs done against it" (1 Cor. 13:5).

(LP) Work on Yourself

This is a big one to curb. When we become obsessed daily about what others, even family members, have done to us, it can eat away at our peace. Of course, there are exceptions to this rule, where bodily harm or emotional duress have been perpetrated on us. Those take a little longer to resolve and could involve some therapy. But in a lot of cases, it might have just been words exchanged that weren't delivered or received in the right way.

When that ugly thought pops up, and it can on a daily basis, hit it with this phrase: "The wrong that has been dominating my life these many years—*that...stops...today.*"

Like most of us, I was bullied in my youth. And it's no joke when you have to approach the school from different doors in hopes of avoiding your bully. With me, I have always been a joy-filled person. Even when I was very young, I knew it was a special gift that most loved but a few hated—like the guys. But it was always attractive to the girls.

One day I was coming home from school and a group of older guys surrounded me and pushed me against a fence. One stepped forward and said, "Hey, man, my girlfriend likes you." I almost said, "With that breath of yours, I can see why!" But I kept my cool and said, "Oh, is that right?" He said, "Yeah, that's right!" Then he punched me in the chest. Then they started arguing among themselves about what they wanted to do to me. So, when I saw their confusion, I thought that would be the perfect time to slip away like Jesus did and head toward the house.

Well, as I tell my group of youngsters, when things like this happen to you, especially after you have made the authorities aware of your situation—*work on yourself!* And that's what I did. I became more dedicated to my music and the possibility of its success.

Years passed and my band and I were doing a concert in Chinatown one night, and the bullies were trying to get in. I had a split decision to make. I decided to let them in because I had a good friend with me, Floyd Piper, who I knew that if anything went down, he could handle the whole group by himself.

Needless to say, all the hard work I had put into my music had now become the bridge. And it's funny, but one of those bullies has become one of my good friends and lives near me here in Vegas. Do I remember the "wrong" done to me? Yeah, sometimes. But the *hidden treasure* is that, it doesn't dominate my life anymore because I put my time and energy into *working on myself!*

> "It never stops trusting, never loses hope, and never quits" (1 Cor. 13:7).

(LP) Too Legit to Quit

Now that is a great attitude to have. It offers power, remedies, and gives a positive spin to everything. Like an Olympic swimmer that severed her spine and lost feeling and movement from her waist down, she was being interviewed the other day and she said, "I'm grateful to still be alive."

You, mothers, embody that same "no quitting" attitude, like a Jesus prototype. You are a constant reminder that His Blood never quits flowing from Calvary, all the way up to our last breath.

We can draw strength from people that have had that same attitude like Martin Luther King Jr., Mother Teresa, Mahatma Gandhi, Col. Harland Sanders (Kentucky Fried Chicken), Henry Ford, and Ella Patillo. All have great stories of never quitting. You should read each story on the web. It will be a *hidden treasure*, encouraging dreams and a reminder to *never quit.*

"So these three things continue: faith, hope, and love. And the greatest of these is love" (1 Cor. 13:13).

(LP) Love: The Glue That Holds All Mankind Together

So at some point we won't need *faith* because we will be with faith Himself, we won't need *hope* because all that we've been hoping for has finally come to pass, but *love* is the true constant from the beginning of time and throughout all eternity. It is *the glue that holds all mankind and life forms together*. If love were at the base of all things, look at the benefits we could derive from it:

No more wars, so young families won't have to worry about a loved one not coming home.

No more poverty, because everyone would share with everyone else.

No more pride, because everyone would be helping the other achieve their individual goals.

No more race issues, because we would realize that each race has something to contribute that the other doesn't have and we would celebrate and be inspired by that difference.

The *husband and wife* would be entrenched in it. Husbands, serving, and the wife, honoring.

Love would cause the *children to* give more respect and appreciation for their moms, dads, elders, and those in authority.

The *planet* would benefit because the human race as a whole would do what's best for Mother Nature so as to leave a richer environment for future generations.

If love were at the base, *teachers* would be more engaged and challenged by exploring all aspects of what a child needs—for his mind, for his body, and for his soul.

I so honor and love my teacher, Mrs. Hughes, because she was the first one to spot the musical gift in me. And I know how important the teachers are because of all the time they spend with our children during their waking hours.

A teacher has an incredible balance to keep, between hearing a student's grievances but not trying to replace the parent, discussing a scenario where there is no father in the home, laying out a curriculum for a latchkey kid where one or both parents work long hours, a nutrition program for the underweight and overweight, a food group along with supplements and alkalized water that could contribute to a child's stamina and health.

One day I hope we will be able to have a book that gives our children and grandchildren a list of moral behaviors. I think we could call it *Love Notes*, like don't kill, don't steal, and don't mess with someone else's boyfriend or girlfriend. A subject matter on bullying, sex, and drugs. All these would be helpful to most students. There are core areas of what makes them tick, and many of us would love to see some of these needed subject matters added to our school curriculum as oppose to what date Christopher Columbus discovered America. Because as we know, if that subject matter comes up, the whole story should be told about the thief of the Indian land and African slavery. Instead of it being all about the noble acts of Columbus, let the teacher tell the whole truth that slaves were brought to this country from Africa against their will and Indians were killed and their land stolen, and stole most of the continent of Mexico.

I think the kids could handle it, and it would help them understand what they are facing in some neighborhoods daily, like when parents split up or divorce and the tension that develops between race and ethnicity.

I believe teachers come to this planet with a special type of psychology in their soul anyway. They have to be educator and part shrink. We all can agree that they are way overworked and underpaid. But we all are so proud of their hearts and the impact they have on our little ones. And I salute you today, especially you, Mrs. Hughes. God used you to put in motion the whole fabric of my life.

If these types of subjects were presented and discussed, I believe our children and grandchildren would be more engaged and there would be less suicides and overall chaos haunting our little ones. I think it would be especially helpful for the bully who's acting out because of a lack of love and attention.

And last, love would create the overall understanding of the *horizontal and vertical lifestyle* and how both are necessary for a full and balanced life. Even though there is a separation between church and state, I don't think anything would be wrong with giving children a list of *"Moral Standards to Live By-Love Notes."* It's about as vertical as we can get without being religious.

This is just a small list of freedoms that love gives us access to. We can also add to this list by ministering to the ones God has given us an audience or favor with: Donate to a cause we believe in; for me, create a new genre of music for the next generation; put our testimony on Facebook and social media outlets; or write a book, to name a few.

The world is a body of people who function more effectively with a strong heartbeat, and I have to take a minute here to mention a few, a chosen few: Like the *military*, in light of my father giving his life for our country at age forty-seven; the *medical professionals*; *law enforcement*, *the clergy* and its *missionaries* around the world; our precious *teachers* that have access to our most precious natural resource, our children; *passionate people* from all walks of life who contribute to the present and future welfare of our nation and planet. Love shows up when ordinary people exhibit extraordinary displays of love. Big shots were little shots that just kept on shooting. Love is our most precious and powerful *hidden treasure*!

Luke 9

When you travel, don't take a walking stick. Also, don't carry a bag, food, or money. Take for your trip only the clothes you are wearing. When you go into a house, stay there until it is time to leave. If the people in the town will not welcome you, go outside the town and shake the dust off your feet as a warning to them." So the apostles went out. They traveled through all the towns. They told the Good News and healed people everywhere.

—Luke 9:3–6

(LP) Hospitality Is a Valuable *Hidden Treasure*

It's interesting how Jesus commanded, even those closest to Him, to depend upon the graciousness of the host in towns they were going to. It is so like that with our ministry. There are times when we have to be alone. But there is a great need to invite fellowship into our life experience. I must say that it is a new experience for me—staying in people's homes. But the exchange of our stories and testimonies are so rich.

This may be a tiny testimony in light of everything else we've been covering. But on one trip to Oregon we stayed with a pastor and his wife. I generally don't like to impose on people because I might break into a song in the middle of the night and wake up the whole neighborhood, dogs and cats included. On this occasion we were about to leave, and they gave us some alkaline water to take on the rest of our tour. I told Renee that I felt something different, like I had more energy and I was more alert. Even in the work out area of the hotel, I was pumping more weight.

I got home and called the pastor back and asked him what he put in that water. He told me the water was processed through a machine that the Japanese have been using for forty years. In fact, it was being used as a medical equipment in most of the hospitals over there. He said he shared the water with his congregation, and those who drank the right amount have been helped especially those with degenerative diseases.

Needless to say, I bought three machines—one for the house to drink, one for the shower that feels like mineral water, and one for the road. I've turned my whole family and friends on to it, and it's been helping them with some of their lifelong health issues.

This all came from doing what Jesus asked me to do, which was to stay in homes.

I probably couldn't count all the blessings I've missed from staying in a hotel. Although I do hear dogs howling outside my window in most places, I'm sure most hotel guest wish my *hidden treasure* would stay hidden.

> "When the apostles came back, they told Jesus what they had done on their trip. Then he took them away to a town called Bethsaida. There, he and his apostles could be alone together" (Luke 9:10).

(LP) Gratefulness

This is a good attitude to develop when one goes out to minister. Come back and throw ourselves into the arms of Jesus and tell Him how *grateful* and appreciative you are for the ministry success that took place.

I have had a habit for many years of going into the bathroom when I get back to the hotel so I don't disturb my family during my time of appreciation. And it's there that I thank the Lord for that night's activities, revelations, transformations, and healings. At least, He knows that I know that He is the Star of the show, not me, who continues to be the *hidden treasure* below.

Jesus continued to say to all of them, "Any of you who want to be my follower must stop thinking about yourself and what you want. You must be willing to carry the cross that is given to you every day for following me. Any of you who try to save the life you have will lose it. But you who give up your life for me will save it. It is worth nothing for you to have the whole world if you yourself are destroyed or lost. Don't be ashamed of me and my teaching. If that happens, I will be ashamed of you when I come with my divine greatness and that of the Father and the holy angels. Believe me when I say that some of you people standing here will see God's kingdom before you die." (Luke 9:23–27)

(LP) Sold Out

This is not only deep but hard to fit into today's prosperity language, which by the way, I'm a big fan of, given the poverty mentality some have tried to persuade us to believe. If we put Jesus in the center of everything we are about and seek Him first, He promised *all* the things that we need would be added to our lives.

With all our getting, if we can in turn give, then that's the kind of vessel God can use for greatness. For example, I think back to the Billy Graham era. He had every tool at his disposal like a rock star but stayed centered with all his wealth, health, good looks, and success.

When someone is *sold out* concerning his or her assignment, it's the best life one could have. And even if we would have made another choice, who is to say that one would have been successful anyway or that we would even be alive to enjoy it.

For instance, in my line of work as a music artist, there have been, and continue to be, many roads one can travel morally. And it really comes down to knowing which one you've been assigned to and have been gifted and equipped to handle. For instance, this new genre of music, through Positive Pop Records, is my biggest challenge to date. I still get nervous presenting the message to a totally non-faith based environment. The biggest blessing though is that it's doing great things for the youngsters.

I have one song called "Rise above the Bullying, Jam." One verse teaches the bullied how to deal with bullies. The second verse speaks to the bully as to how he can redirect his energy. Then it wraps up with the chorus line taken from the title.

One teenager shared with me that he has to listen to this song at least once a day to be able to deal with those kids who are bullying him. It's gratifying to know that if we stay in our lane, even though we may feel unqualified to accomplish the goal, God has a way of using our gift and making us relevant for His purpose. *Sold out* is another *hidden treasure*.

> "The time was coming near when Jesus would leave and go back to heaven. He decided to go to Jerusalem. He sent some men ahead of him. They went into a town in Samaria to make every-thing ready for him. But the people there would not welcome Jesus because he was going toward Jerusalem. James and John, the followers of Jesus, saw this. They said, 'Lord, do you want us to call fire down from heaven and destroy those peo-ple?'" (Luke 9:51–54).

(LP) I Was Taught to Always be a Bridge

This is a good scripture to remind us how Jesus would want us to be with people of different beliefs and or just plain rejecters of us and our message. We all need to work toward being *a bridge* between people, because love is really *the* solution for all mankind's woes. "We are known and read of all men." It means that what they sense from us is the vibe they will get concerning the One we're representing.

I remember a season with my friend and colleague Carlos Santana. We would have lots of conversations about spiritual things more than anyone else in the group. One time I was at his house playing tennis and the conversation came up about Jesus coming back and what would we say to Him concerning the blood sacrifice He made for our sins. I mentioned to him what I did when confronted with the question. I told him, "It was suggested to me to make a confession of faith to our precious Savior. Then get baptized as an outward expression of that decision." I was pleasantly surprised when he said that he'd like to do that too!

So I set things in motion with my pastor friend, Bob Pagent, at the Assembly of God Church on Mission Street in Santa Cruz, California. It was a glorious day filled with tears of joy watching the music warrior make his verbal confession and get ducked down into the baptismal pool.

We never know who we will be in conversation with that we don't even think would be moved by what we say or believe. I do know that whoever we share with will have a peace in their heart that wasn't there before. And if we truly love our neighbor as we love ourselves, we would want them to have what my friend Joel Osteen would call their "best life now." A true *hidden treasure*.

Luke 10

After this, the Lord chose 72 more followers. He sent them out in groups of two. He sent them ahead of him into every town and place where he planned to go. He said to them, "There is such a big harvest of people to bring in. But there are only a few workers to help harvest them. God owns the harvest. Ask him to send more workers to help bring in his harvest.

—Luke 10:1–2

(LP) Many Hands Make the Work Light

If there was ever a question about if we are to call on more folks to help in our ministry, this scripture clears that up. Thank you, Lord, for your confirmation. We can boldly ask, seek, and knock now, knowing that our God has made these arrangements and has His wind at our back. And, personally, I have faith that everyone I ask will contribute something to our children's outreach and new genre of inspirational music and they will appear when the need arises. According to scripture, *"Many hands make the work light."*

I really enjoyed the part that Findlay Toyota played in our children's outreach. Not only financial assistance, but they become good friends. When the GM (Rich) passed away two years ago, we all rallied together as a family. I think that unexpected tragedy brought our hearts even closer.

After Rich went to be with the Lord, I counseled with my financial friend of the company. And he suggested Subaru of Las Vegas. Come to find, it's the same company Rich began with years ago and the GM was excited to be a part of this new chapter. So I am happy to announce that I am their new celebrity spokesperson. Many *hands are working together* to give the GM, employees, and customers God's best.

> But Jesus said to the apostles, "You give them something to eat." They said, "We have only five loaves of bread and two fish. Do you want us to go buy food for all these people?" There are too many! (There were about 5000 men there.)
>
> Jesus said to his followers, "Tell the people to sit in groups of about 50 people."
>
> So the followers did this and everyone sat down. Then Jesus took the five loaves of bread and two fish. He looked up into the sky and thanked God for the food. Then he broke it into pieces, which he gave to the followers to give to the people. They all ate until they were full. And there was a lot of food left. Twelve baskets were filled with the pieces of food that were not eaten. (Luke 10:13–17)

(LP) God Never Wastes Anything

And again, on a personal note, being in partnership with an Asian woman, leftovers are the norm. Every year I sing at the Metro Police Department's fundraising gala here in Vegas. Catering serves all of us huge pieces of steak. No way in one sitting could I consume the whole thing! Last year I asked our waitress if I could take it to go! She just laughed at me. I didn't see what was so funny at $5,000 a table. Looking through the eyes of my Filipino wife, that was a negligent waste. Leftovers are *hidden treasures in your field.*

Of course, this speaks to our life experiences as well. Some may be good ones; some may have experiences that you wish you could forget. But Scripture says, *"God causes all things to work together for our good, for those who love Him and are called according to His purpose." Nothing wasted!*

God loves giving us more than we deserve. Why? Who knows! But it makes me think about the blood He shed on Calvary. That one act of love I will never waste.

> "They answered, 'Some people say you are John the Baptizer. Others say you are Elijah. And some people say you are one of the prophets from long ago that has come back to life.' Then Jesus said to his followers, 'And who do you say I am?' Peter answered, 'You are the Messiah from God.' Jesus warned them not to tell anyone" (Luke 9:19–21).

(LP) Who Do You Say That I Am

Who do you say that I am? What a question? Even philosophers and scientists are searching deep space to answer that one. The simple answer is that you, Jesus, are the Savior of the world, as evidenced by the sun. We always say how beautiful it is to see the sun rise or the sun set, which makes it look like the sun is moving. But actually, the earth is rotating around the sun, not the other way around.

And along that same thinking, when the sun catches the clouds just right, they turn a beautiful shade of red that even a poet like myself would find hard to describe. I do sense, though, that when the Father is looking down on earth and the sky is like that, it reminds Him of His Son's sacrifice and His heart is reminded and warmed toward His creation. Because of the way we have been acting of late, it's only His grace that allows us to experience another day of life. "From the rising of the sun, until it's going down, the name of the Lord, shall be praised. Since the beginning of time, until thy kingdom come, the name of the Lord shall be praised. Blessed be the name of the Lord!" That's who I say that you are.

The other morning I woke up with an acronym for the word GRACE. *And on a sidenote, I wonder why God always wakes me up at four in the morning. Maybe I was supposed to live in another part of the country. But I must admit, it promotes a quiet time when my day's activities haven't started to bombard me yet.*

The acronym for *GRACE* is GIANT REBELLION, ALL CANCELLED, ERASED. That to me is God's grace. GIANT REBELLION, ALL CANCELLED, ERASED. Some may say, "Yeah, Leon, you've had quite a rebellious life." But me, I have what I would call a general rebellion. Then my question would be to you, Do you ever feel like poppin' your husband upside the head for no reason? That might be a giant rebellion to him.

In the face of this revelation and knowing that our Savior could take us out for any negligence on our part and choosing not too is pretty compelling. I know when someone crosses me, I'm not so eager to forgive and could hold it over their head for longer than they deserve. So when I'm asked about, *Who do I say that He is?* I say, "A God of grace," *a hidden treasure in the field.*

And you, my fellow warrior, are a spring in the desert, a light to the world, one put *way* up on a hill for the whole world to see. You are connected to the One in the center of our universe that holds us all together. Don't ever forget that. *Amen.* And that's who I say you are.

Back to Luke 10:

> When the 72 followers came back from their trip, they were very happy. They said, "Lord, even the demons obeyed us when we used your name!"
>
> Jesus said to them, "I saw Satan falling like lightning from the sky. He is the enemy, but know that I have given you more power than he has. I have given you power to crush his snakes and scorpions under your feet. Nothing will hurt you. Yes, even the spirits obey you. And you can be happy, not because you have this power, but because your names are written in heaven." (Luke 10: 17–20)

(LP) Whose Foot Is on Whose Neck? Part 2

I'm so glad Jesus cleared that up. I had heard it preached a few times that we were under the foot of darkness because of Adam and could never rise above that curse. Come to find, according to this scripture, the enemy will strike at our heal but ultimately his head would be under Jesus's shoe that causes me to look at this demonic thing from a different angle. If Jesus has got His foot on the head, the rest of the body becomes immobile, especially concerning our ultimate destiny and afterlife experience, as the scripture below confirms.

"You will bite her child's foot, but he will crush your head" (Gen. 3:15).

Some years back I used to accompany my friend and fellow colleague Bob Larson. He is known in our circle as the demon buster. On one occasion we were in Anchorage, Alaska, at a huge Baptist church and Bob spotted a guy in the audience who was manifesting. He called the man forward and asked him about his life. In a loud voice the gentleman was shouting out about worshiping an Earth God. So Bob yelled back for the demon to come out! It was something I will never forget because when Bob said that an earthquake occurred! The chandeliers were swaying, and the pews had folks sliding from side to side. My son Douis, who had never witnessed anything like this before, abruptly got up and ran out of the church, followed by his mom. I thought about leaving too, but I was playing the music!

The man then fell to the ground and started rolling around. It was something out of the *Exorcist* movie! I had been with Bob for a while at that point but never saw anything quite like that, especially with the earthquake and all!

After the meeting, I asked Bob if he had ever experienced anything like that before. He told me that strange things always happen when he's confronting dark forces.

The first time something like that happened to me was in a concert at the Music Hall in Houston. Not as dramatic, but a woman was yelling during a few of my songs. From where I was on stage, she seemed to be enjoying the concert. But when I stopped singing to greet the audience, she was still yelling. I knew then that she was trying to disrupt our time together. So I spoke right into the mike and said, "You, Spirit of division! I command you right now to be silent! You will not have your way in this concert, because this concert has been anointed and appointed by or Lord Jesus Christ!" The whole time I was speaking, she was still yelling until I said the name of Jesus. Then she gave off another scream, then collapsed in her seat. This invigorated the audience, and they started chanting the name of Jesus. Since then, there have been a few outbursts from time to time. But it continually reminds me that dark forces are out there, as the scriptures say, "to kill, steal and destroy." And we as believers have to step up and say, "Not on my watch!"

Bob always reminds me that a lot of it is just Psychology 101 as I discovered on another occasion in Dallas where we had men stand up that had been sexually assaulted growing up. Out of two thousand in the audience, half of the men stood up. Bob explained that people plagued by that growing up tend to be so traumatized, that a spiritual imbalance can set in. In some severe cases, a dark side will begin to develop and gain momentum through the years.

I pray for you today that God will touch and release you from the dominance of such a spirit. And I speak to this thing that has haunted you every day of your life to leave your body right now, in the name of Jesus. That you will stand up and begin to fight back against these forces of evil with God's Word. "That no weapon formed against you will prosper!" That you will no longer see yourself as the tail—but the head! Never again being the lesser but the bless-er of life and mankind! Time now, Lord, to create in me a clean heart and renew a right spirit within me! You are the Alpha and Omega, the beginning and the ending of all things! And right now, Lord, I order the death of this improper dwelling in me and continue to move toward your glorious light! For the path of the righteous is as the light of dawn that shines brighter and brighter until the full day. My life will be full of your Light, my Savior! That light is transforming me right now! I will make a miraculous recovery so much so that people will think I must have got a new hairstyle. It will be obvious to my family, my closest friends, coworkers and new acquaintances. New, all new and ready and willing to pursue this new chapter in my life! Constantly uncovering new and exciting *hidden treasures in my field*!

Then an expert in the law stood up to test Jesus. He said, "Teacher, what must I do to get eternal life?"

Jesus said to him, "What is written in the law? What do you understand from it?"

The man answered, "'Love the Lord your God with all your heart, all your soul, all your strength, and all your mind.' Also, 'Love your neighbor the same as you love yourself.'" Jesus said, "Your answer is right. Do this and you will have eternal life." (Luke 10:25–28)

(LP) Eternal Life Is Simple to Achieve

It's funny how complicated we make everything with so many doctrines and philosophies when the base of it is all about loving God and loving others as you do yourself. I'll practice that, Lord, in all I do and in every situation I find myself in, which is illustrated below:

But the man wanted to show that the way he was living was right. So he said to Jesus, "But who is my neighbor?"

To answer this question, Jesus said, "A man was going down the road from Jerusalem to Jericho. Some robbers surrounded him, tore off his clothes, and beat him. Then they left him lying there on the ground almost dead.

"It happened that a Jewish priest was going down that road. When he saw the man, he did not stop to help him. He walked away. Next, a Levite came near. He saw the hurt man, but he went around him. He would not stop to help him either. He just walked away.

"Then a Samaritan man traveled down that road. He came to the place where the hurt man was lying. He saw the man and felt very sorry for him. The Samaritan went to him and poured olive oil and wine on his wounds. Then he covered the man's wounds with cloth. The Samaritan had a donkey. He put the hurt man on his donkey, and he took him to an inn. There he cared for him. The next day, the Samaritan took out two silver coins and gave them to the man who worked at the inn. He said, 'Take care of this hurt man. If you spend more money on him, I will pay it back to you when I come again.'"

Then Jesus said, "Which one of these three men do you think was really a neighbor to the man who was hurt by the robbers?"

The teacher of the law answered, "The one who helped him."

Jesus said, "Then you go and do the same." (Luke 10:29–37)

(LP) Love Sweet Love

I love how Jesus put his messages in story form, showing us how to apply heaven principles. I like that the Samaritan made contact with the victim by cleaning up his wounds and, in contemporary terms, put him in his car and drove him to the nearest Holiday Inn, where he paid for his hotel stay for a season. It also goes to show that if someone is displaced that you don't necessarily have to bring them to your home, as long as your heart makes a way for their need. Now that's lovin' your neighbor.

I've just recently wrote a song about a "Bridge." I was born and raised in San Francisco and there are three bridges that interconnect the Bay Area. Lyrics to the chorus part says,

"I was taught to always be a bridge…
stretch for those, who're out there…
on a ridge. I was taught to always be a bridge…
to help someone across, that's my privilege."

We covered a lot of this in the love section above, but suffice to say, all of life hinges on loving God and our neighbor as ourselves. This is the *hidden treasures* of life. If the contributions we are put here to deliver could be seen through the eyes of love, every gift would make such an impact that darkness couldn't even get up out of his chair. Light will always dominate the darkness—no matter how dark it gets—because we have love and light Himself, living in our heart, ready to activate at a moment's notice, if we can just stop, take a breath before we react to any situation. Whenever in doubt, give love. The *hidden treasure* everyone needs and is in search of.

What does the song say?

"What the world needs now is love sweet love.
It's the only thing that there's just too little of.
What the world needs now is love, sweet love.
No not just for some but for everyone!"
(Burt Bacharach).

What a *treasure*-filled song.

> "But the Lord answered her, 'Martha, Martha, you are getting worried and upset about too many things. Only one thing is important. Mary has made the right choice, and it will never be taken away from her'" (Luke 10: 41–42).

(LP) The Journey Is Where Most of Life Is Spent!

It's good to take a few moments and listen to what the Lord wants to share. Take time to meditate during the day, just to reflect on what is really real. The destination is important, for sure, but *the journey is where most of the life is spent.*

Renee and I spend a lot of time on the road, and a lot of folks ask, "How can you be away from home for so long?" My answer is surprising to most, and it's simply this: "Home is wherever we are."

I have an acronym for the word *PURPOSE*: Pure U, Reflecting Pop's Optimism, Stamina, and Essence. Toward the end of the book, I have a mini sermon on the subject. I hope you will pick up a lot of *hidden treasures in your field*.

This is the key to unlocking our potential. Our purpose also gives us a day-to-day reminder because it's natural for us to forget. We are a species that constantly have to be reminded. Even in the time of Jesus, the disciples forgot after feeding five thousand people when they were challenged to feed four thousand. The destination is important for sure, but *the journey is where most of the life is spent*.

Luke 11

One time Jesus was out praying, and when he finished, one of his followers said to him, "John taught his followers how to pray. Lord, teach us how to pray too." Jesus said to the followers, "This is how you should pray: 'Father, we pray that your name will always be kept holy. We pray that your kingdom will come. Give us the food we need for each day. Forgive our sins, just as we forgive everyone who has done wrong to us. And don't let us be tempted.'"

—Luke 11:1–4

(LP) Prayer: The Ultimate Weapon

Teach me what you want me to teach my disciples, Lord, especially these children who are looking to me to drop seed in their little hearts. May I never fail to take a moment to listen and listen deep to their goals and challenges! Give me your wisdom and instinct to accomplish what you have called me to do. It is my privilege and my honor to serve them and you, oh Lord.

The beginning episodes of "Sing Children's Foundation" was very memorable. We had just moved to Las Vegas from Southern California in hopes of retiring or at least cutting my concert schedule in half, maybe 80 concerts instead of 160 a year. My pastor friends Randy Greer and Vic Caruso called and informed me that they had just lost their music minister. The Assembly of God's assistant director and my good buddy Sam Huddleston told Pastor Randy that I had just moved to town and could possibly help out. What was supposed to be a cut back was now potentially a schedule increase. As the

Lord would have it, during the time I was helping out, Rich, the GM of Findlay Toyota, and his wife, JoAnn, would come and sit right in the front row. He really enjoyed the music presentation because he was a fan from years before.

During these beginning stages of absorbing this new city and environment, I heard all the stories about the spiritual attacks on the city, especially the main one being on the kids. Come to find, Las Vegas had the highest dropout rate in the whole country. Mom and Dad would always have foster kids in our home. In retrospect, that must have made a subliminal impact on me because as soon as I left the Santana band, I started doing the same thing.

So as I stated before, I helped Koinonia with their quest for twenty plus years. And even though I was thinking about retirement, my little heart was drawn toward helping children again. I began to pray about how we could divert the hearts and minds of these youngsters toward the arts. Pastor Randy must have known I would need help with this new venture and kept pushing me to start up a friendship with the GM. It was a marriage made in kid-sponsorship heaven. Rich had the heart and the resources to help me provide a positive outlet for this type of mission. As I stated before, Subaru of Las Vegas has now stepped up to continue this legacy.

As we venture into this new genre of music, Lord, help me to be faithful to this next level. Even though I only had five years with my friend Rich before he came to join you, continue his legacy. Send helpers to join with me on the frontlines. Help this new relationship with Subaru, and my new friend and GM, Burton Hughes to be productive for the sake of children and their parents. They, along with so many other friends and fans, are helping our most valuable resource, the kids, to experience *hidden treasures in their field*. What a powerful tool prayer is. It's an invisible weapon that you have given to mankind that allows us to present to you our needs and concerns and then confirmation after confirmation coming from your word, answering before we ask, as we continue: "But he will surely get up to give you what you need if you continue to ask. So I tell you, continue to ask, and God will give to you. Continue to search and you will find. Continue to knock, and the door will open for you. Yes, whoever continues to ask will receive. Whoever continues to look will find. And whoever continues to knock will have the door opened for them" (Luke 11:8–10).

(LP) Continue

As you can see in this passage, *continue* is used a lot. I'm sure you're like me sometimes in that you start something but distraction comes along to trip you up. Most of us get it during prayer time. Oh, how we want to stay focused in prayer, but inevitably, all our day's activities comes barging in. With me, as soon as I notice the shift, I immediately begin again until my soul is satisfied. In fact I had a confirmation of a tool that can be used when our mind falls into a pit: 5–4–3–2–1. I use it in my new song "Ready 2 Rise." The concept is simply that, as soon as procrastination sets in, re-trigger yourself by saying out loud "Five–four–three–two–one," then continue with the task at hand. Even a wonderful lady named Mel Robbins mentioned it on YouTube. This is a great *treasure* to have at your disposal for anything, anywhere, any time. That will re-trigger you *to continue*.

Continue, my friend, you are so close to accomplishing your God-given goals, even though it may seem to take longer than you expected. Keep pursuing it because it is running just as fast toward you!

It's an honor to swallow my pride, Lord. My part of the bargain is to trust you enough to know that what I do in the secret place will eventually come out in the light. A lot of us take that secret place as a negative, like whatever mischievous thing we do in secret we hope others don't learn about. But let's flip the script—the good we do in secret will hit the light with an even greater force.

My daily prayer is that the Lord will make me relevant, that what I do in my life will *continue* to hold significance. Obviously, if you're reading this book, that prayer is being answered in real time.

I have discovered that when you get older, you must reinvent yourself. It's somewhat like the universe. Scientists say that it's expanding, or it could be that what's already out there is slowly being discovered as our technology increases. I think our Lord's plan for us is to keep learning, keep climbing, keep reaching. The good news is that there is enough *hidden treasure in our field* that we will never run out of ideas and contributions, even if we had a hundred lifetimes this side of heaven. *Continue, my friend, continue!*

> Every kingdom that fights against itself will be destroyed. And a family that fights against itself will break apart. So if Satan is fighting against himself, how will his kingdom survive? You say that I use the power of Satan to force out demons. But if I use Satan's power to force out demons, then what power do your people use when they force out demons? So your own people will prove that you are wrong. But I use the power of God to force out demons. This shows that God's kingdom has now come to you. (Luke 11:18–20)

(LP) God's Family Protection Plan

This again makes clear that any entity that takes a crack shot at somebody's family is out of line. And if a family member does it, like someone in the body of Christ, that's really disgusting. We must always be on guard against this because, in actuality, it is not a flesh-and-blood fight but principalities and powers in dark places that provoke it. But I like verse 20:20, *"But I use the power of God to force out demons,"* a major but secret *hidden treasure*, as we continue below:

> "When a strong man with many weapons guards his own house, the things in his house are safe" (Luke 11: 21).

(LP) Guard Your Heart from Creeps

This is another way of saying guard against things that start *creeping* its way into our heart. Before we know it, it's running our house and life instead of JC. That's especially true here in Vegas, with its many options and creature comforts. But, personally, I think you see more skin on the beach than here. At least a few people have clothes on.

I remember one season in my life when things were a little tight financially. During that time, I went to visit Mama Doll in San Francisco. Parked in front of the house was a brand-new Cadillac! I don't know about you, but there are times when the desire for a thing becomes quite compelling. Well, I immediately started to pray a prayer to God to give me a vehicle just like that.

A few months passed, and I ran into an old friend who was one of the top salesman at a Cadillac dealership in Long Beach, California. I thought, *Wow, Lord, you could not have answered my prayer with more confirmation than this.* So as you can guess, with a ridiculously low down payment, due to my friend's ingenuity, I drove off in a brand-new luxury Cadillac.

But because my work had slowed down considerably, I couldn't keep up with all the maintenance needed and the car started to show wear and tear way ahead of its years. Also the car note was making me work more hours than I wanted, which resulted in less time for my spiritual and family routines. I say all this to say, *Guard your heart from creeps.*

The attraction to have a thing can always be justified, but is it really a God thing? We can ask and have it in the same breath, but is it in our best interest? So looking back at my experience, I should have also prayed for the payments and maintenance money. God wants us to get the most out of this life because He came to give us life and that more abundantly. But we must always be willing to put those last few words at the end of our prayer, "If it be thy will." That is a *hidden treasure* that will help us not get blindsided even by our own desires. *Guard your heart from creeps.*

"Whoever is not with me is against me. And anyone who does not work with me is working against me. They ask for a miracle as a sign from God. But no miracle will be done to prove anything to them. The only sign will be the miracle that happened to Jonah. Jonah was a sign for those who lived in Nineveh. It is the same with the Son of Man. He will be a sign for the people of this time" (Luke 11:23, 29–30).

(LP) Signs Are Everywhere

Lord, let me be a sign for this time. I might not be the greatest example (flawed as I am), but my vessel continues to be at your disposal. Every generation needs the witness of Christ so that the gospel can continue through the ages.

Like the many words you have encouraged me with through the years: "Springs in the desert;" "Glory of the present house, greater than that of the former;" "Faith, the assurance of things *hoped* for, the *evidence* of things *not seen*;" and "Foreigners will rebuild your walls." Such words have created *signs everywhere*.

I pray that your presence will so dominate the arts and science that it will be mandated to explain in the classrooms. It won't even be seen as religion but a phenomenon that will have everyone mesmerized and investigating, like *hidden treasures* waiting to be unearthed—a *sign!*

I must admit that when I was approached by Richard concerning my faith, it wasn't altogether foreign. But I only related to Christ in the religious sense, like Christmas and Easter, but not to actually have a relationship with Him. It's like a child finally waking up and realizing all the sacrifices their mom and dad have made for their existence.

If you were to really think about it, my friend, I'm sure *you* could make a personal list concerning all the times you felt His hand on your life. In fact, that might not be a bad idea to go back as far as you can remember and let each experience and story just flow out of you. You could even use social media as one possible outlet and turn it into a testimony. It would give an un-refutable *sign* to future generations!

That is how this book began. And when I looked at the scriptures in the book of Luke, so many experiences just flooded my soul.

One personal experience was during my twenties. I had a group called Leon's Creation (which after fifty years has just released our album, *This Is the Beginning* on a label out of Europe called Acid Jazz, but don't laugh at my hairstyle and clothes, it was a seventies thing).

My bass player friend and band director Jimmy Calhoun always found a way to book us into clubs. One club he booked was in San Jose, California, where he lived. It was only a fifty-minute run from San Francisco but seemed much longer after performing from 9:00 p.m. to 1:00 a.m., then packing up and leaving around 2:00 p.m. One night I had a few angel visits on the way home. I had put my all into the performance that night and celebrated after with a few spirited drinks. In retrospect I should have crashed on Jimmy's couch, but I used my mom's car and had to get it back for her to use early the next morning.

I have heard of people blacking out when they drink and not remembering much from the night before, but I was doing that as I drove. It was as if every time I looked up at a freeway sign, I was miles down the road, without knowing how I got there. This went on until I got within five miles of my house. And as they say, that's when things go to pot. No pun intended.

As I was making the last turn on the freeway, I must have really dosed off because I could hear scraping on the driver's side of the car. It startled me, so I sat straight up in my seat and rolled down both windows.

All along my ride home, I realized I had been dozing off. And I believe with all my heart that Christ assigned an angel to guide my car, me not crashing or getting into a serious accident. Is just like one of the *signs* that speak to me today about His destiny for my life.

When I woke up the next morning, my mom was shaking the bed and asking me to come with her. She showed me the side of the car where the molding was missing and asked me what happened. Being quick on my feet, I said, "Mama, we were in a bad neighborhood last night, and somebody must have stolen the molding." She knew I was lying, but it must have hit her funny bone because, she started laughing, almost uncontrollably, while hitting me upside the head. Just like Jonah and the fish, it was a *sign* to me that something else was at play that night. And I sure thank Him for assisting me with the steering wheel.

I'm sure as you look back over your life, you will remember testimony after testimony about miracles He has performed for you. *Signs* are *hidden treasures in your field*. Share them so they won't just follow you into the dirt nap!

> "On the judgment day, you people who live now will also be compared with the people from Nineveh, and they will be witnesses who show how guilty you are. I say this because when Jonah preached to those people, they changed their hearts and lives. And you are listening to someone greater than Jonah, but you refuse to change!" (Luke 11:32).

(LP) Change: A Constant

This scripture is a great reminder that one of the major foundation stones of this life is change. And those of us in ministry are constantly promoting change. But funny enough, us teachers of God's truths need it first so we can see even clearer into the lives of those God has entrusted us with.

The Jewish priest of old had the same challenges. To give you an overview, you should read Leviticus chapter 16. The gist of it is that, during the time of atonement, the priest would take two bulls. The first would be sacrificed for the sins of the priest and his family. The second would have the sins of Israel placed on him and then led out and set free in the wilderness. The scary part is how we allow our lives to resemble Israel in the desert—just going around and around and around because they wouldn't *change*, doing the same thing over and over again and expecting a different result. But we have a power far greater who has made an investment in us for our future, and we've got to "make that *change*," like the performer Michael Jackson reminds us.

During the writing of this book, we have just elected the forty-fifth president of the United States. He, like most people seeking this office, is promising a *real* and much-needed *change* for our nation. I hope that he will have the support of Washington to make the necessary adjustments to help our land. And we offer up a prayer today as the scriptures encourage us to do. May his decisions and the decisions of Congress be in our best interest as a nation. And may you bless the USA and the whole world to seek after your face with a whole heart. It is our prayer today and down through the ages that mankind will *change* in a way that will reflect a God visited heart.

It wouldn't take much to fix us, just the light that God has placed in each one of us, shining together. I see our brightness—not like a glare, like trying to look at the sun—but the light would be more like a presence. Not glary and harsh, but valor or iridescent, pleasing to the eye and inviting to the soul. To the point below...

> "No one takes a light and puts it under a bowl or
> hides it. Instead, they put it on a lamp stand so that
> the people who come in can see" (Luke 11:33).

(LP) Light It Up!

This has been my goal and continues after over forty years with Jesus. There are so many oil wells in my backyard that I'm overwhelmed with options and opportunities and favor. God, you are so good to me and so consistent. As I look back at the five-thousand feed and the four-thousand feed, I am reminded of the many peaks and valleys you've brought so many of us through. It was and is the grace of God that truly sustains our lives.

I believe that the choice to volunteer for a frontline position in contemporary Christian music in the eighties was the best place I could shine from. It was risky, being that there were no drums being allowed in the churches in those days, which challenged us to do concerts in regular halls like the mainstream groups did. It was a real challenge to convince a promoter to take a chance on investing in a hall, publicity, and such for something that had never been tried up to that point. Plus, after all that, would people come?

But I knew "Light on the hill" was my goal, as scary as it was. The Lord put a fire under many of us, and that fire still burns today in some way. I'm so proud of the generation that stepped up to the plate after us. Even one of my sons, GabReal, who's with Toby Mac are playing some of the same halls I did, using some of the same promoters! The *Hidden Treasure* is that whatever environment we find ourselves in, "Light it up."

When I do my "Rise above Bullying" rallies, I bring my first gold album so the middle school and high school kids can get pumped up. Plus, it gives them a reference because most of them have never heard of Santana—but all their grandparents have! LOL! But I tell them that we all have a special God-given gift inside of us that we can turn into gold. Scripture says it another way: "The same one who made what is outside also made what is inside. So pay attention to what is inside. Give to the people who need help. Then you will be fully clean" (Luke 11:40–41).

(LP) Small Things Make Big Things Happen

The constant daily needs of people's souls are just as important as any missionary outreach. Jesus put it this way: *Thy word is a lamp to my feet.* Meaning, the intricate details need to be attended to, just like the big stuff. In the eyes of our Lord, it is just as important and means just as much as the big stuff. I can't tell you how many small checks come into our ministry, but they come…right…on…time!

I remember a time when we were making a major outreach investment and we had literally exhausted all our savings in hopes that God would turn things around in this nation. Even as a seasoned veteran, sometimes I have doubts, all the way up until it manifest. It was like that on that day.

When I went to the mailbox and saw an envelope with the small see-through plastic window, I went, "Great! Another bill." I don't know what possessed me to open it and read it, but I did. And to my surprise it was God's gift to us. The credit card company almost doubled our credit limit! But more than that, it was a confirmation, again, that His Eyes are always upon us and His ears are open to our prayers. Small things are the epitome of a *hidden treasure.*

Luke 12

Then Jesus said to the people, "I tell you, my friends, don't be afraid of people. They can kill the body, but after that they can do nothing more to hurt you. I will show you the one to fear. You should fear God, who has the power to kill you and also to throw you into hell. Yes, he is the one you should fear."

—Luke 12: 4-5

(LP) No Fear

These words to me, on a personal tip, say, "Don't just be an entertainer. Revolutionize the industry you have influence in." If you stop to ask everybody what they feel or think, except for your private council, you will end up going on an emotional loop because everyone has an opinion, which is their right to have. But you have one too, especially if it's a God-ordained direction or mandate.

The biggest challenge of my career was when I was at a loss as how to deliver this wonderful God-given music. I thought about a band, but that meant I would have to pull families into my commitment. Earlier in my career, the concerts couldn't justify a full band unless we were going to live out of a bus, year-round. So, fortunately, there was a new technology that came out that allowed me to program my show on a computer. It was the Oberhiem System, which assigned each instrument to a different computer box. I programmed and rehearsed with this new delivery of music for four months, then decided to take it on the road.

My first concert was in Perth, Australia, where I heard that the people there were very forgiving. The promoter, David Smallbone, assured me that everyone would be in awe of whatever came out of this new presentation. So my engineer and I flew there with seventeen anvil cases worth of gear.

The first night was magical in the sense that no one had ever done anything like this in the world. And the Aussies were going to be the first to experience a one-man band. I had written a song called "Star of the Morning," and that was one of the songs they were playing heavily on the radio, so I started with that. Three computers were synced together and triggered by a remote pedal at my feet. The plan was to start off playing the piano, building up to a crescendo, and then hitting the pedal that would trigger all three computers. Well, I did the buildup, hit the pedal, and nothing. I did it again... and nothing. Of course, the fans didn't notice. To them it felt like it was building toward something.

What had happened was, I was so nervous that when I would hit the pedal to trigger the computers, I was turning them on, then turning them off again. I knew, if all else failed, I could trigger the computers with the manual button. I tried that and the sound of French horns and strings began to fill the auditorium. I could tell, as everyone was looking in amazement, that they expected a full orchestra to emerge from behind the curtain, except there was no curtain and no backstage.

Needless to say, the challenge was well worth the risk. I knew after that experience that I could travel all over the world as a solo artist and the fans would experience a feeling of a band and orchestra. You never know what you can accomplish till you try.

No fear is definitely one of those *hidden treasures*. Second Timothy 1:7 (ERV) says, "The Spirit God gave us does not make us afraid. His Spirit is a source of power and love and self-control." *No fear...No fear...No fear.*

> "When birds are sold, five small birds cost only two pennies. But God does not forget any of them. Yes, God even knows how many hairs you have on your head. Don't be afraid. You are worth much more than many birds" (Luke 12:6–7).

(LP) You Are Worth Something

For those who suffer from a feeling of worthlessness, this is a good scripture. Even if nobody gets you, God does, and lets us know again that we are important and valuable to the one that really counts. It is so refreshing to hear this today. It clears the air on so many levels—doubts; fears; insecurity; nationality; calling; job description; marital status; singleness; height and weight; communication skills; likes and dislikes; joys and hobbies; family background; personal background; abilities; past, present, and future goals and failures; and tons of other mental challenges that bombard us over the course of our lives.

To know that I'm *worth something to God* is huge, because nobody else's opinion really matters (like I said, except council and definitely your wife).

This is my mantra to the youngsters: *You are worth something.* I even wrote a song called "Rise above the Bullying, Jam." Many have hit me on Facebook and said that they like it. Like we did, they experience bullying in school and it continues as one grows up, in the work place and on social media.

We have a middle school not far from where we live, and there was a beautiful, bubbly little thirteen-year-old girl who was being bullied at school and a lot on social media, so much so that she decided to go into the downstairs bathroom that she shared with her mom, dad, and little sister and hang herself!

If only we could get a message of "worth" to these kids, we could interrupt this horrible epidemic.

A message of hope or even a song that says, *"You are beautiful and you matter."* And before they know it, those words of affirmation will cause them to see themselves differently. Maybe Grandma and Grandpa could take 'em to church and help guide them into the arms of Jesus. *Worth* is another one of those powerful *hidden treasures* that can reverse the constant cruelty from the dark side.

> "I tell you, if you stand before others and are will-
> ing to say you believe in me, then I will say that

you belong to me. I will say this in the presence of God's angels. But if you stand before others and say you do not believe in me, then I will say that you do not belong to me. I will say this in the presence of God's angels" (Luke 12:8–9).

(LP) More Than a Material World

I am not ashamed of the Gospel because it is the power of God unto salvation to those who believe. Yes, Lord, we try and do some powerful stuff in our own name. But what breaks through is the power source already put into motion by you, oh Lord. As we enter in, let us be mindful of the power grid in prayer, in humility, in service, in the spoken Word, in the delivery of a great song or speech. You are par with every communication tool man can come up with, because in reality, it existed in your mind before it was even created down here on earth. Mankind is the one who strives to stay in step with your revelations.

When we uncover another one of your *hidden treasures*, (1) we have unlimited power at our disposal, and (2) it opens us up to future activity that is present in the spirit realm and waiting to materialize. But only through belief and association with you can this be accomplished.

I believe that realm of possibility was made aware to Zuckerberg, Gates, Buffett, Sister Teresa, Billy Graham, Martin Luther King Jr., and Oprah to name a few. An appointed season in time that a human was entrusted with God-like persona to show everyone what is possible. Those people alone should rattle us out of our complacency because they are mere humans. Hardworking humans, I grant you, but flesh and blood all the same.

Even though you have allowed me to have some success and influence in this world, it would all be a waste if I didn't have you, my God. It is an honor to be chosen to follow Jesus.

Life is more than the material world. The feeling of knowing that little eleven-year-old Loretta was affected so by the words of one of my songs that it caused her to make a physical change that everyone could see. The loss of her fifty pounds continues to reverse her being bullied at school. And at the appointed place and at the appointed time, she acknowledged you, oh Lord, as her personal savior. And within a few months the same Savior rescued her dad—now that is the most powerful *hidden treasure* of all.

> "When men bring you into the synagogues before the leaders and other important men, don't worry about what you will say. The Holy Spirit will teach you at that time what you should say" (Luke 12:11–12).

(LP) An Honest Tongue Brings Freedom

I experienced this in Wentzville, Missouri, right before midnight at a concert on New Year's Eve. I got up and shared from my heart during the last five minutes before the balloons dropped. I was truthful and honest about some past struggles and how God forced me into a counseling time that saved my life. It was revealing, informative, and instructional—and no one will ever forget what was shared that night. Yes, it was a chance-taking experience, but during my whole speech, I could hear the Father's voice reminding me that "the truth shall set you free."

God can give spontaneous words of inspiration, if we are willing to open our mouths and be transparent. Most of us think that our experiences are so unique, that no one else could relate. Come to find we all struggle with a lot of the same issues. And if any of us are bold enough to admit some stuff, it would help others swim stronger through their storm of challenge and insecurity. Your experience is my experience and a *hidden treasure in our field*.

> Then he said, "I know what I will do. I will tear down my barns and build bigger barns! I will put all my wheat and good things together in my new barns. Then I can say to myself, I have

many good things stored. I have saved enough for many years. Rest, eat, drink, and enjoy life!"

But God said to that man, "Foolish man! Tonight you will die. So what about the things you prepared for yourself? Who will get those things now?"

This is how it will be for anyone who saves things only for himself. To God that person is not rich. (Luke 12:18–21)

(LP) Re-Fire

This is the first time I noticed a scripture that addresses retirement. According to this scripture, it sounds like we need to stay in the game, or at least stay active in some way. I have seen instances where people retire and just sit around on the couch all day. It seems like a wonderful experience at first to relax and do nothing, but the body was made for activity. And when it doesn't receive that in some way, the mind and the muscles start to atrophy.

I have a cousin that was really looking forward to retirement. He worked at the post office and would explain to me that if he worked a few more years, he would gain more income for his retirement. So he decided to work a few years more. Then he and his lovely bride moved to a country setting in California and began his retirement, which included mostly lounging and such. He would call me and tease me about still working so hard in my ministry, and I have to say, the way he would explain what he did every day did tempt me sometime. Well, after six months, he went to the doctor for a general checkup and the doctor told him he had stage 4 cancer.

It was a sad day for me when I got the news that I was about to lose my relative and best friend. He and I had experiences that a lot of cousins never share, starting from childhood, straight through marriage, children, and the death of our parents. The greatest of our experiences together happened when he came to a concert of mine and gave his life to Christ.

So my word to retirees is to take all these years of wisdom and find a place to give some back. You may be retired but still find a way to stay active and relevant. A good example is the movie *The Intern* with Robert De Niro. His wisdom and insight helped to save a company. He was retired, but he re-fired!

Just when the world says we are of no further use, the Lord is reminding us again to continue giving and sharing. It is a true *hidden treasure*. I hope this gives you a lot of energy today to know that our work is not in vain in the Lord. In my world, I still have his approval and anointing to keep, writing, recording, performing, releasing books, and ministering right up until the day that He calls me home. Re-fire, Grandma, Grandpa!

> Jesus said to his followers, "So I tell you, don't worry about the things you need to live—what you will eat or what you will wear. Life is more important than food, and the body is more important than what you put on it. Look at the birds. They don't plant, harvest, or save food in houses or barns, but God feeds them. And you are worth much more than crows. None of you can add any time to your life by worrying about it. And if you can't do the little things, why worry about the big things?
>
> "Think about how the wildflowers grow. They don't work or make clothes for themselves. But I tell you that even Solomon, the great and rich king, was not dressed as beautifully as one of these flowers. If God makes what grows in the field so beautiful, what do you think he will do for you? That's just grass—one day it's alive, and the next day someone throws it into a fire. But God cares enough to make it beautiful. Surely he will do much more for you. Your faith is so small!
>
> "So don't always think about what you will eat or what you will drink. Don't worry about

it. That's what all those people who don't know
God are always thinking about. But your Father
knows that you need these things. What you
should be thinking about is God's kingdom.
Then he will give you all these other things you
need." (Luke 12:22–31)

(LP) Our Father Knows All We Need

Boy, that says it all doesn't it? The part that is most engaging is
verse 30, "*That's what all those people who don't know God* are always
thinking about." That right there puts me in check. Am I always
thinking about that one subject matter—money and the many
"material things" of this world? Good question, Lord!

The Lord is saying to us not only to not worry, but that he will
so take care of us. That we will appear more beautiful than the flow-
ers of the field—and I have seen some pretty landscape in my travels
throughout this awesome country. So again, if we just focus on God's
Kingdom, *all* that we could ever ask or think will be available to us.

One warning, though, and this will be a *hidden treasure* for you
today. What will become available to you are houses, lands, cars,
clothes, toys, etc. But remember, you have to pay for them. So you
have to ask yourself, "Do I want to work that hard to have all those
things, or do I want to have a simpler, more meaningful life that has
more peace attached to it?" It's only a question, my friend.

I share this from the back nine of my life. Now that I am here,
I can look back and see what some of the true highlights were. Places
and people where I put too much time and places I wished I had put
more time. If you can balance things out to really have a quality life,
you won't just be existing but really living the "abundant life" God
promised. And it continues some more below.

Don't fear, little flock. Your Father wants to share
his kingdom with you. Sell the things you have
and give that money to those who need it. This
is the only way you can keep your riches from

being lost. You will be storing treasure in heaven that lasts forever. Thieves can't steal that treasure, and moths can't destroy it. Your heart will be where your treasure is. (Luke 12:32–34)

(LP) True Treasure Is Put in People

This scripture is loaded with goodies and good to know that when we put our treasure into people, it can never be spent. I can attest to the fact that money comes and money goes, and sometimes we have nothing to show for it. And not only will our *treasure be well spent putting it into people*, but it gains equity to be distributed to generations to come.

That's one of the reasons why a person like Martin Luther King Jr. and many like him were on such a mission. They knew from early in life what true treasure was. The cool part is, if we continue down this street for the rest of our lives, the *treasures* we have dropped in people's heart will never disappear or be stolen. No one, not even the dark one, can take them away.

I have a message called You…Are…On…Assignment, and I always tell my fans across the country that any assignment you're on, if it's less then what Shadrach, Meshach and Abednego were assigned to do, you're cool. Even the inconvenience our Lord had to go through on the cross for us is way less than most of us will ever encounter.

If we keep thinking about planting our treasure in lives, it will keep us centered and fired up! We'll be surprised at how many *hidden treasures* will be unveiled on that day!

Be ready! Be fully dressed and have your lights shining. Be like servants who are waiting for their master to come home from a wedding party. The master comes and knocks, and the servants immediately open the door for him. When their master sees that they are ready and waiting for him, it will be a great day for those servants. I can tell you without a doubt, the master will get himself ready to serve a meal and tell the servants to sit down. Then he will serve them. Those servants might have to wait until midnight or later for their master. But they will be glad they did when he comes in and finds them still waiting. (Luke 12:35–38)

(LP) Getting Ready 'Cause Here I Come

I have a friend who was trusting God for a special business he wanted to begin.

But it hasn't come to pass yet. And somewhere along the way he concluded that God didn't hear his prayer and he walked away from the faith. I recently saw a movie like that as well, *Miracles from Heaven*, which had this same type of theme.

Our job is to wait until midnight or *later* for the fulfillment of God's promise. I know it can be challenging but as stated above, "They will be glad they did…"

A time beyond where we think He might not show up. But show up, He will. It's in Scripture, and those words never return void without accomplishing what God desires.

"Many of people have given up, they say the pressure is too hard to bear. Don't have to do it all by yourself, someone cares, up there. No one else but you, can do exactly what you do…so let your talent come bursting, right on through…because the Sky is the limit…you can reach, beyond the stars…Sky is the limit…let yourself go, let His river flow!" *Get ready, get ready, get ready!*

When I got the call from Carlos Santana to audition for his group, I had been performing, writing, and living with my band, Leon's Creation. It was an unexpected call, but all my lights were on. Even after I had joined the group, Carlos gave me a whole day in the recording studio to teach his group my new song, "Mirage." Each band members' part seemed to come so effortlessly because of the arranging I had been doing for Leon's Creation and many others in Hollywood. "*Getting Ready 'Cause Here I Come*," I'm sure the

Temptations will be surprised to see their song being used to illustrate a biblical principle.

I have even seen "getting ready" in older people that get the urge to date again. They start dieting, exercising, and finding social events to attend in their age group. It's the cutest thing to see. I just recently ran into a couple that told me what a joy it was to finally meet the one they had been praying for. They went online to a Christian dating site, and when they met, they both were surprised to encounter exactly what they had hoped, prayed, and prepared for. "Get ready" is a sweet hint from our Lord and a unique *hidden treasure*. And it continues. "What would a homeowner do if he knew when a thief was coming? You know he would not let the thief break in. So you also must be ready, because the Son of Man will come at a time when you don't expect him!"

(LP) Stay Ready

I heard a story once that's connected to this scripture, and it's this: When a guy saw a thief break into his house, he went down stairs and got his weights. (You thought I was going to say gun, huh?) Nope, he got his weights and started working out! Yep, that's funny! That's why we must pick up our cross and follow Him daily. So when the dark one comes to kill, steal, and destroy, he won't rob our house because we've been hitting the spiritual weights on a consistent basis.

From 1999 till 2012 I traveled with a group called the Get Motivated Seminars headed by my friend Peter Lowe. It began with Peter attending an outreach that our mutual friend Bob Larson was doing. As Bob's musical guest, Peter got a chance to see me in action. When the event was over, he approached me about performing at his seminars. At first I couldn't see how I could be of use, especially since my songs were mostly church oriented at that time.

I thought Peter's meetings were going to be in a hotel ballroom with about three hundred to six hundred people. But he informed me that our first one together would be at the Great Western Forum, the old arena of the Lakers in LA. I said, "Whaaaat!" It really challenged me to look through some of my repertoire of songs to see if anything would fit for his group of mostly sales people.

Even though it was not a religious seminar, most of the attendees knew that I had gone from Santana to Hosanna! And I explained to them that because of my Catholic wife, I had to change the words to some of the hits.

When the music would start, some would stand and dance. Others would just clap from their seats or just sway along with the music. Then the lyric would come out, "I had a black magic woman...I had a black magic woman...I had a black magic woman... but she got saved, sanctified and set free. Now I've got a born-again woman keepin' the devil off of me!" At the end of that line, everyone would always give a rousing applause.

Who knew that so many songs from the past could be altered a bit and create such a perfect musical atmosphere. Sometimes we're ready, and we don't realize it. Maybe at our time of challenge, all we need is a little altering. The Holy Spirit is always right on time, with a nudge in the right direction concerning our gifts, especially if it is going to glorify the gift giver.

Stay ready, my friend, a *hidden treasure* that continues. "Who is the servant that the master trusts to do that work? When the master comes and finds him doing the work he gave him, it will be a day of blessing for that servant! I can tell you without a doubt, the master will choose that servant to take care of everything he owns" (Luke 12:42–44).

(LP) You Have a P. U. R. P. O. S. E.

Now I see why God-gives certain responsibilities to certain ones. I admire a lot of people who have really put forth the effort to achieve what they have. And I ask myself, would I have given that much to it? And then I look at what I have committed to, and others are most likely saying the same thing about me. Of course, us men, have more of an admiration club then you women.

That's why it's important to throw our arms all around our assignment. We have been tempered for it, selected for it, our talent lines up exactly perfect for it, and, most of all, God anointed and sanctioned it.

Another word that we need to digest, if we are to make a lasting impact with our gifts is the word *purpose*. You can skip this explanation until later, but I think the explanation for *purpose* will be the glasses through which everything else will be evaluated.

Pure U - is a state of being, with your own fingerprint, totally unique out of the billions of people that are born, which should be a driving force behind anything you set your heart on doing.

Reflecting Pop's - like the moon does in reflecting the sun's light. It's interesting to note that the moon has no light except the one the sun gives it. That's volumes of books right there.

Optimism - regardless of what the five senses reveal to us, our optimism has veto power, like the president does. Everyone else is seeing one thing and, surprise, out comes the unseen that you knew instinctively would happen. When our mouths confess optimism, our ears hear it and the brain tells the flesh. Then you have massive fighting power at your disposal over any opposing voices or forces!

Stamina (which could actually be a play) - stay the course like Joseph did on his way to the palace. Joe grew up with eleven other bothers who were more worker types with no dreams, visions, or motivation toward the future. On the other hand, Joe was a visionary and was not afraid to share his dreams and visions with family members or friends. And because Joe was next to last of Dad J's children, he felt a little closer to Joe. They were all farmers by trade, and one day Daddy J sent Joe to check on his brothers who were grazing cattle miles away from the ranch. When Joe caught up with them, a continued hatred came on all his eleven brothers.

I believe that one of the triggers that set the eleven brothers off was a special coat that Daddy J had given to Joe. It was thick, long, and colorful. And I imagine as Joe rolled up on his brothers in that coat, the bothers could not take another moment of what seemed to them to be an apparent cockiness. Joe always knew he was different from the rest, and I assume that his walk reflected a stride of superiority and swagger. They spontaneously rushed him and threw him into a nearby well, but the brothers thought about their action and decided to ship him off to another part of the country. I'm sure Joe hated to be shipped off like that, but thinking about dying at the bottom of a well, another city was definitely, a better alternative.

This could be played out for the public schools if the subject comes up about religious parallels. Simply say, it's just a coincidence, like most movies or plays that have a lot of commonality. (I would love to narrate or have one of the respected voices of the church narrate. The actors in the play wouldn't have lines but patterned movements based on the narration, which could be entertaining, comical, as well as informative)

Essence - is a flavor that you give off that reflects the thing, person, or entity you are connected to. People are drawn to it because it represents *thee* life force.

Back to Joe: Well, Joe entered his new life as an administrator for a high executive in his new metropolitan city with buildings as high as the sky. It was a far cry from the little country town he came from. After a short period of time, his boss noticed Joe's essence. It was a confidence he carried concerning his upbringing, his administrative skill set, and his faith.

This immediately placed Joe in the upper echelon of the company, and before long, he was the one running the show with the boss's blessings. But Joe still had a longing for home. In the back of his mind, he remembered his dream of being in a position one day that would cause him to oversee thousands and thousands of people's lives. So he focused on the job assigned to him, and he did it as if thousands were depending on him for leadership.

Of course, one of the areas of *stamina* that is always challenged is integrity. And as time passed, he was confronted by Mrs. Boss. Joe was a handsome man. Like his brothers, he was always out in the field, which gave him a pleasant golden tan. And dealing with field animals ten to twelve hours a day can develop muscle tone that not even the gym could provide. And, as previously stated, Joe was intelligent, morally sound, a visionary, and single, which made him attractive and irresistible to almost any female!

One day Mrs. Boss decided to tempt her fate and see if this gorgeous man would succumb to her approach. But as you would expect from a man put in his position, he thought it highly immoral and indecent to be the lover of another man's wife. Of course, after so many attempts and rejections by Joe, her pride was hurt and the spoiled brat that she was began to surface.

One day, as Joe stormed out of the house in disapproval of her most forward approach, Mrs. Boss decided she would get back at him by lying to her husband, that Joe had been approaching her. This made the boss so mad that he had Joe arrested, charged with attempted rape, and sent to jail.

Joe must have questioned everything at this point. If he was to be the head of some great movement or company one day, how was a jail sentence going to look on his resume? And where was his guiding light in all this? Were all the dreams just a figment of imagination? After all, the visions he had seen as a child were so vivid and different from everyone else he knew, including his family. Was this whole thing just a fantasy?

But being a man of *stamina*, he set his mind on the tasks ahead and offered his talents and services to the warden. Before he knew it, here he was again, being entrusted with a position of leadership under the warden. And everything that involved his *purpose* came through in his work, so much so that the warden and staff had a much smoother operation in the prison system because Joe was in charge.

One day the president of that country was upset at two of his most trusted employees—the butler and the wine connoisseur. He decided to punish them both for their impropriety and insubordination. They were indicted, found guilty, and were thrown into the same prison as Joe. It was like a white collar crime, so the sentence was not as severe as a violent one.

One night these two convicted felons had dreams; and Joe, being the head jailer, was very intuitive when it came to a change of mood on the compound. So he asked them what seemed to be the problem. Was it the food or sleeping arrangements? They responded that it was neither one. But they both confessed, almost simultaneously, that they had dreams that they could not figure out. Joe, being a God-fearing man, seemed to have insights that had developed over time from prayer and meditation. He asked them to share their dreams and maybe Jehovah could help him interpret!

The wine connoisseur started first, and when he was over, Joe said, "In three days you will be restored to your job." Being encouraged by Joe's answer, the baker gave his story, and Joe said, "In three days you will leave prison too, but you will be hanged." I'm sure the baker wished he had never asked Joe anything. But Joe, being quick on his feet, asked the wine connoisseur to intercede for him with the president. However, when the wine connoisseur got back into position, he forgot all about Joe.

Joe knew that he was being called and trusted with a great responsibility, but with each day he must have felt like, "When, Lord? When, Lord?" Then finally, after two years, a call come to the head jailer that the president was confused about a dream he had. When that happened, the wine connoisseur remembered that his cell mate could interpret dreams. So Joe was cleaned up and was presented to the president. One thing that he knew was he had to get this one right. He was wise to tell the president that these sort of explanations and interpretations came from God, not him, which I thought was wise from any angle. After the president told him his dream, Joe knew right away what it meant and proceeded to offer the president solutions that would no doubt save the presidency and the country.

Because of the overwhelming display of *purpose* on Joe's part, he was elected to the vice president position. Not only did all that he had envisioned come to pass, but he was *Pure U* in the process, with his flavor being added to the mix, *Reflecting Pop's*, which he did every step of the way in a country that didn't even respect his belief system. *Optimism* in that he could sense that God's words would never return void. *Stamina*, which gave Joe the strength to endure, until his *purpose* could unfold. *Essence* to glorify the Lord, concerning revelations and dreams, which allowed everybody in the land to "taste and see that the Lord is good!"

May God's *purpose* be evident in everything we do because it's a real guiding force to why we're here. *Purpose* is a *hidden treasure in your field.*

> *Who is the servant that the master trusts to do that work?* When the master comes and finds him doing the work he gave him, *it will be a day of blessing for that servant! I can tell you without a doubt, the master will choose that servant to take care of everything he owns. (Luke 12:42–44)*

(LP) A Life Well Spent

This is the beautiful end result of a life lived in serving. As we all know, loving God and loving our neighbor are the two greatest commandments. According to this scripture, we are already blessed and will obtain eternal life just in doing that. But, if God feels like we can handle more, then that's a maxed-out life. I have felt shades of that with a few humble accomplishments. And if the things I've done outlasted me and there is fruit in heaven too, oh man, then I know my God is pleased and I will have had a life well spent—what a *hidden treasure.*

> "Whoever has been given much will be responsible for much. Much more will be expected from the one who has been given more" (Luke 12:48).

(LP) There Is Still More

Help this to be true, my Lord, that you are happy with all you expected for me!

This is truly a step of faith, investing in souls. But what a wonderful day it will be when we arrive in heaven and see all the fruit of our labor! When so many approach us with words of gratitude for paving the way for them being there. I have always made a habit of giving my audience something to think about as I leave the stage. I do it in a more personal style now as opposed to having them get up and come down front, but the impact is still lasting.

Just recently I heard from a forty-year-old man named Paul from Australia who told me that he went to one of my concerts at age thirteen and it set in place the pathway for his life. Before his encounter with me, he was a guitar player but after seeing the concert, he immediately switched to piano and has been using his gift to make a living that way for all these years. The big thing was, at that concert, he made a confession of faith and is now spreading his love for Jesus in a secular environment.

I have shared my faith in God since 1974, and I know I have received greater responsibility. But as I approach even greater challenges, I feel like my journey is just beginning. So as an encouragement to some of you who have been on this trail as long, or even longer than I, you too have been given more to carry and my prayer is that you carry it well.

Our Father in heaven is so proud of you. Straighten up that back. Raise your head high. Breathe in a fresh wind of the spirit today. Take one more big step of faith, knowing that our Heavenly Father continues to entrust you with responsibility, honor, and valued leadership. As long as there is breath in those lungs, there are still more *hidden treasures in your field*!

> "Jesus continued speaking: 'I came to bring fire to the world. I wish it were already burning! There is a kind of baptism that I must suffer through. I feel very troubled until it is finished. Do you think I came to give peace to the world? No, I came to divide the world! From now on, a family of five will be divided, three against two, and two against three'" (Luke 12:49–52).

(LP) Family: The Battleground

I see this with Abraham's family, between Ishmael and Isaac. The promised child was Isaac, but God said He would bless Ishmael as well. The conflict continues even till this present day. I asked a highway patrolman friend, if drive-bys were the highest forms of killings in our country. He said, "Nope, homicide is." I was surprised. "You mean family members and close friends killing each other?" He said, "Yep! The state of our world is broken from within."

I see this problem as a communications issue. I have a teaching that helps with this dilemma, and I call it CHAIRS—a place where those who love each other can take time to be open and honest. It's a teaching that I go into later, and it is literally saving lives.

I have two precious friends that have decided to get married, and we've been having premarital discussions. The relationship was going along fine for about two years. Then in the last two weeks before the wedding, all hell broke loose. I told them that it's a spiritual attack that I see all the time. Even though he's in the West Coast and she is in the East, I told them to make a point to pray together morning and evening. And God's power would help them to ultimately overcome the attack. Well, happy to report that they have continued with their plans and the fiancé just went to her final dress fitting today.

Regardless of what we as a family are struggling with, the family is the battleground and is constantly under assault. I think the Wikipedia gives a good explanation for assault: "In criminal and civil law, assault is an attempt to initiate harmful or offensive contact with a person, or a threat to do so. It is distinct from battery, which refers to the actual achievement of such contact." It's a good explanation because it's a taunt by the dark side to do something and a lot of it is just being played out in our head. We haven't been physical struck by anything. Please take time to read CHAIRS just below. It plays out a familiar story that will help you create a defense mechanism. A very in-the- moment *hidden treasure*.

> "'It will be bad for you, you experts in the law! You
> have taken away the key to learning about God.
> You yourselves would not learn, and you stopped
> others from learning too.' When Jesus went out,
> the teachers of the law and the Pharisees began to

give him much trouble. They tried to make him answer questions about many things. They were trying to find a way to catch Jesus saying something wrong" (Luke 12:52–54).

(LP) Don't Be Caught Off Guard

The key to life is to be constantly learning and improving. It is part of the spiritual and physical growth process. If we have at least a glimpse of what to expect when approaching a job, a school, a home-based business, and even marriage and children, no one can catch us *off guard!*

During the week, I not only read passages from the Bible, but also from self-help books from many famous motivational gurus of our time. It may seem unorthodox to expand a career later in life, but we keep hearing it over and over again, "You're never too old to learn." For example, when I turned fifty, I stepped up my exercise program. It has given me more stamina on stage and in my home life. God will always reward us in accordance to what He stretches us to do. If we go deeper with Him, we will function on a deeper level. We even initiated a season of fasting and prayer, which never is the most fun thing. But we have found that a lot of things that would *catch us off guard*, we can smell coming way ahead of time.

I am not afraid of the task ahead because *you* called me to it before the foundations of the world. Even the creation of this book, *Hidden Treasures in Your Field.* Though it was a challenge to do, the content will last way beyond my years. I pray it will touch a generation of people that I will never get a chance to meet on this earth. I hope it will help in motivating people to continue unearthing the ground around them in search for life's *hidden treasures.*

Lord, I pray that you encourage those looking on to be inspired to believe you for more exciting and meaningful experiences. As the Karen Carpenter song says, "We've only just begun—to live." I encourage you, Grandma, Grandpa, your wisdom alone can refocus a household, a neighborhood, and indeed the world—even from a bed or a wheelchair.

The book you read last night will be sifted and interpreted through the many years of your experience. When you tell the story of what it means to you, the lights will come on for somebody. When you meditate on God's word and convey its deeper meaning as you see it, may it reset a generation that doesn't even know where the reset button is. It's hard to catch someone *off guard* when they have their hand on the pulse of life, Christ Jesus. Even rereading His ancient words will strike you in a new part of your heart. And no matter how young or how old you are, you can never be caught *off guard* meditating in that book.

You, my friend, have the right to speak, simply because you're here. Remember, in the beginning of your life, "you outran the millions that were chasing after you," toward fertilization. Well, your wisdom and life challenges have shaped you in such a way that you can be a better *guardian*—and more sophisticated GPS systems! You are simply a one of a kind *hidden treasure* that the world should take time to excavate. They'll be surprised at what they will discover! Someone who is hard to knock *off guard!*

> A father and son will be divided: The son will turn against his father. The father will turn against his son. A mother and her daughter will be divided: The daughter will turn against her mother. The mother will turn against her daughter. A mother-in-law and her daughter-in-law will be divided: The daughter-in-law will turn against her mother-in-law. The mother-in-law will turn against her daughter-in-law. (Luke 12:53)

(LP) CHAIRS: A Communication Tool

I should have known God is behind everything. Nothing goes on that He is not aware of. But when you bring up the name of Jesus, especially at family functions or work, there can be a resistance in the air. I thought it was me. Nope, it's just the way things are. To not be afraid of the rejection is just the posture we must take. You dig in and let everybody else squirm. In other words, be a thermostat instead of a thermometer. You regulate the temperature in the room.

The story that has changed lives:

Below is a scenario that I put together to describe a situation that happens to most couples:

It's a beautiful Sunday morning, and you and your wife have decide to go to the early service so you can be first in line for lunch at your favorite restaurant. When you come into the church, the music is very inviting. In fact, it's the Sunday that they are playing all your favorite songs. You can even close your eyes and sing without using the side screens.

When the pastor takes the stage, he starts off with a prayer that is so stirring that even the hardest hearted person goes into self-reflection. Then he smoothly segues into his message that is a subject that you and the wife have been discussing for a season—without any real resolve. The message was so informative that after the service you could hardly wait to get to the gift shop to pick up a copy.

As you leave church you and your better half are holding hands and smiling as you greet members on the way out. And since it's a nice day, not to cold not too hot, you decided to put the window down a bit to catch a breeze on the way to your favorite spot.

As you pull up in the parking area, the valet guys rush to both sides of the car and greet you like you're the restaurant owners. You both jump out as white birds simultaneously took off and fly right in front of you. It's like a scene out of a movie. So you take her hand, smile, then stroll into the foyer.

Even though the restaurant is full of people waiting for a table, the maître d' sees you coming in and immediately opens up another line so he can take you to a seat next to the window overlooking God's grand estate. There is nothing that could possibly ruin such a perfect moment.

The waiter comes and gets your drink and lunch order as he sets down complimentary appetizers, the chef's pick. You thank him and take each other's hand again as you sigh and turn toward the beautiful view.

Then something happens that periodically happens when there's little conversation and things are quiet. One of you come up with a subject matter that you didn't quite finish talking about the last time you visited this tension-bearing subject! And as it was the last time, here it comes again.

By the time the waiter arrives with your food, no one's talking or holding hands. Butts are turned up to each other, staring in the opposite direction, and checking cell phone messages. You even argue over who's going to pray over the meal.

"Are you going to pray?"

"No! I prayed last time."

"No, it's your turn to pray!"

"Okay, okay, okay! Jesus wept! Now let's eat!"

The food is the most wonderful smelling dishes you've ever experienced. But you can't taste a thing because the preceding conversation is still rotting in your mouth. After lunch you walk out, not saying good-bye to the nice waiter or maître d'. You get into your car and don't tip the valet and then turn the heat up all the way, hoping the other one burns up. Sound familiar?

This kind of situation is begging for *CHAIRS*! So the set up for this fix is this: Go to a part of the house that you don't frequent much like the dining room, hallway, or the garage. The reason for this is so you don't associate any negative emotions and conversation with the rooms that you experience joy in, like the kitchen or bedroom. You set up two chairs, facing each other, and you begin your dialogue. It would be good to let the woman go first, unless there is a dispute where the man has obviously been wronged.

This is a space, where there is no holds barred, a space where you can communicate everything that you have been keeping bottled up inside. This is where you can share all your resentments, disappointments, or anything that makes your heart cold toward the other. As you share, also picture a third chair with Jesus sitting in it. That always helps to include Him in on your discussion, as well as reaching deep down to come up with the best language to communicate your true feelings, as if you're talking with someone you really love and respect like Mom, the boss, or the pastor of your church.

When the woman starts, the husband's job is to stay quiet until she finishes. A conversation where everything and anything can be discussed.

After the wife has finished, it's the husband's turn to do the same, with her staying silent till he's finished. You may agree to disagree, but what's important is that both of you got a chance to hear the other's grievances.

I remember the beginning of this exercise years ago when Renee and I had a serious disagreement on the way from Long Beach, California, to Palm Springs to play golf with her brother Jerry. We were forty-five minutes out, and I turned the car around and headed back toward the house. Of course, it was quiet all the way back, but when we got our CHAIRS situated, we were able to get everything off our chest! The conversation took about one and a half hours, but it was time well spent.

We still arrived in enough time to have a late dinner with her family. And a beautiful day of golf the next day. Had we not turned around, the conversations with her family would have been a little strained. It still happens from time to time, but if one of us mentions CHAIRS! We know soon we will have an outlet to express ourselves.

I can tell you from experience that things may not change immediately, but the words from the other does make an impact in time. I've slowly transitioned toward the hopes and desires of my loved one, and she has done the same.

Then, the last part of chairs is this: *Kiss*! It may be the most uncomfortable part of the whole exchange. But it puts a loving touch on the ending. We do CHAIRS because the Bible says, "Don't let the sun go down on your anger."

I have heard some say, that they use this technique with their children. In a few cases, coworkers have sat in CHAIRS too! Lack of communication is why some homicides happen. Because there seems to be no outlet for the fury one feels inside. So it's acted out in physical and verbal abuse, even affairs are linked to letting someone else Band-Aid our pent-up emotions. Others may even end up in divorce or even a fatality.

CHAIRS, *a communication tool*, is a *hidden treasure* that has helped to save a lot of relationships; and I pray that it will help you with yours.

Luke 13

Jesus told this story: "A man had a fig tree. He planted it in his garden. He came looking for some fruit on it, but he found none. He had a servant who took care of his garden. So he said to his servant, 'I have been looking for fruit on this tree for three years, but I never find any. Cut it down! Why should it waste the ground?' But the servant answered, 'Master, let the tree have one more year to produce fruit. Let me dig up the dirt around it and fertilize it. Maybe the tree will have fruit on it next year. If it still does not produce, then you can cut it down.'"

—Luke13:6–9

(LP) We're Designed to Bear Fruit

This is my desire for this book—that it will be one of the most *fruit-bearing* plants of my career, to date. There are also other oil wells in me waiting to produce. With the right investors, promoters, distributors, PR, and agent, it will happen because of God's will and the P. U. R. P. O. S. E. of why He made me (Pure U-Reflecting Pop's-Optimism, Stamina, and Essence).

When you think of the many people that have gone before us—all the great success stories never came easy. But with *great seeds* in their heart, they bore more than they thought possible. May the seeds that are hidden in us suddenly come to the surface and cause a field of trees. It's time for us to "Take wings and fly." May these scriptures below become our mantra!

Ask of Me, and I will give You The nations for Your inheritance, And the ends of the earth for Your possession. (Ps. 2:8, New King James Version)

He said to me, "Today I have become your father, and you are my son. If you ask, I will give you the nations. Everyone on earth will be yours. You will rule over them with great power. You will scatter your enemies like broken pieces of pottery!" (Ps. 2:7–9, ETR Version)

Great blessings belong to those who don't listen to evil advice, who don't live like sinners, and who don't join those who make fun of God. Instead, they love the Lord's teachings and think about them day and night. So they grow strong, like a tree planted by a stream—a tree that produces fruit when it should and has leaves that never fall.

Everything they do is successful. (Ps. 1:1–3)

For some of you who have been waiting for a while with no substantial fruit showing. Take a lesson from the Chinese Bamboo Tree.

Keep Watering Your Bamboo Tree
Eric Aronson

In the Far East, there is a tree called the Chinese bamboo tree. This remarkable tree is different from most trees in that it doesn't grow in the usual fashion. While most trees grow steadily over a period of years, the Chinese bamboo tree doesn't break through the ground for the first four years. Then, in the fifth year, an amazing thing happens—the tree begins to grow at an astonishing rate. In fact, in a period of just five weeks, a Chinese bamboo tree can grow to a height of ninety feet. It's almost as if you can actually see the tree growing before your very eyes.

Well, I'm convinced that life often works in a similar way. You can work for weeks, months and even years on your dream with no visible signs of progress and then, all of a sudden, things take off. Your business becomes profitable beyond your wildest dreams. Your marriage becomes more vibrant and passionate than you ever thought it could be. Your contribution to your church, social organization and community becomes more significant than you have ever imagined.

Yet, all of this requires one thing—faith. The growers of the Chinese bamboo tree have faith that if they keep watering and fertilizing the ground, the tree will break through. Well, you must have the same kind of faith in your bamboo tree, whether it is to run a successful business, win a Pulitzer Prize or raise well-adjusted children. You must have faith that if you keep making the calls, honing your craft, reading to your children, reaching out to your spouse or asking for donations, that you too will see rapid growth in the future.

This is the hard part for most of us. We get so excited about the idea that's been planted inside of us that we simply can't wait for it to blossom. Therefore, within days or weeks of the initial planting, we become discouraged and begin to second guess ourselves.

Sometimes, in our doubt, we dig up our seed and plant it elsewhere, in hopes that it will quickly rise in more fertile ground. We see this very often in people who change jobs every year or so. We also see it in people who change churches, organizations and even spouses in the pursuit of greener pastures. More often than not, these people are greatly disappointed when their tree doesn't grow any faster in the new location.

Other times, people will water the ground for a time but then, quickly become discouraged. They start to wonder if it's worth all of the effort. This is particularly true when they see their neighbors having success with other trees. They start to think, "What am I doing trying to grow a bamboo tree? If I had planted a lemon tree, I'd have a few lemons by now." These are the people who return to their old jobs and their old ways. They walk away from their dream in exchange for a "sure thing."

Sadly, what they fail to realize is that pursuing your dream is a sure thing if you just don't give up. So long as you keep watering and fertilizing your dream, it will come to fruition. It may take weeks. It may take months. It may even take years, but eventually, the roots will take hold and your tree will grow. And when it does, it will grow in remarkable ways.

We've seen this happen so many times. Henry Ford had to water his bamboo tree through five business failures before he finally succeeded with the Ford Motor Company. Richard Hooker had to water his bamboo tree for seven years and through 21 rejections by publishers until his humorous war novel, M*A*S*H became a runaway bestseller, spawning a movie and one of the longest-running television series of all-time. Another great bamboo grower was the legendary jockey Eddie Arcaro. Arcaro lost his first 250 races as a jockey before going on to win 17 Triple Crown races and 554 stakes races for total purse earnings of more than $30 million.

Well, you have a bamboo tree inside of you just waiting to break through. So keep watering and believing and you too will be flying high before you know it!

The bamboo tree, a true *hidden treasure*, literally.

Luke 13

Jesus taught in one of the synagogues on the Sabbath day. A woman was there who had an evil spirit inside her. It had made the woman crippled for 18 years. Her back was always bent; she could not stand up straight. When Jesus saw her, he called to her, "Woman, you have been made free from your sickness!" He laid his hands on her, and immediately she was able to stand up straight. She began praising God.

—Luke 13:10–13

(LP) The Bent-Back Spirit Has Left the Building

As I said before, I remember the experience in New Orleans, when the little fourteen-year-old girl got her back healed. We just began praising the Lord, and she stood up erect. I never knew anything like this could ever happen in my concerts, but I was willing to reach out and take a chance.

I performed at a boys and girls club in Sequim, Washington, on my tour. It was a first for me to be back in the club since I was a youngster. During the concert, I could feel an emotional *bent-back spirit* in the room—low self-esteem, thoughts of suicide, and all the other attacks our precious little ones are dealing with. One good thing about our time together was that everybody said it was just what the club needed.

The only thing that broke my heart was not having enough time with them. Come to find, they felt the same way about me. I picked up on it when I signed autographs. Those that had one arm signed came back again and had their other arm signed, then their hand and face. And with each signing, they wanted to have another picture taken.

The neat thing was that *the bent-back spirit had left the room* by the time I drove away. And so, as a maintenance plan, I left my CD *Ready 2 Rise* for them to play throughout the building.

Thank you, Lord, for the healings that most of us can't see. I know that it happens every time I do a concert. And I know that God is touching souls, though many may never admit it.

> "Jesus said again, 'What can I compare God's kingdom with? It is like yeast that a woman mixes into a big bowl of flour to make bread. The yeast makes all the dough rise'" (Luke 13:20–21).

(LP) *Ready 2 Rise*

Sometimes we think that someone or something we have been promised from the Lord will never surface. Then all of a sudden here it comes in full force—proving all the critics of our life wrong again! I say that to say don't give up on your family, your kids, or your grand-kids. Maybe even the dream of being married again—no matter what it looks like in the natural. God has got a plan, like the Chinese bamboo tree, and suddenly, the miracle will happen!

Most of us take Einstein's name as synonymous with genius, but he didn't always show such promise. Einstein did not speak until he was four and did not read until he was seven, causing his teachers and parents to think he was mentally handicapped, slow, and antisocial. Eventually, he was expelled from school and was refused admittance to the Zurich Polytechnic School. It might have taken him a bit longer, but most people would agree that he caught on pretty well in the end, winning the Nobel Prize and changing the face of modern physics.

Orville and Wilbur Wright: These brothers battled depression and family illness before starting the bicycle shop that would lead them to experimenting with flight. After numerous attempts at creating flying machines, several years of hard work, and tons of failed prototypes, the brothers finally created a plane that could get airborne and stay there.

Vice President Dick Cheney and businessman made his way to the White House but managed to flunk out of Yale University, not once but twice. Former President George W. Bush joked with Cheney about this fact, stating, "So now we know, if you graduate from Yale, you become president. If you drop out, you get to be vice president."

After his first audition, Sidney Poitier was told by the casting director, "Why don't you stop wasting people's time and go out and become a dishwasher or something?" Poitier vowed to show him that he could make it, going on to win an Oscar and has become one of the most well-regarded actors in the business.

While today Steven Spielberg's name is synonymous with big budget, he was rejected from the University of Southern California School of Theater, Film, and Television three times. He eventually attended school at another location, only to drop out to become a director before finishing. Thirty-five years after starting his degree, Spielberg returned to school in 2002 to finally complete his work and earn his BA.

In his formative years, young Ludwig van Beethoven was incredibly awkward on the violin and was often so busy working on his own compositions that he neglected to practice. Despite his love of composing, his teachers felt he was hopeless at it and would never succeed with the violin or in composing. Beethoven kept plugging along, however, and composed some of the best-loved symphonies of all time—five of them while he was completely deaf.

Our job is to believe in God and in the one He sent. Plant the seed, and even though some days look like nothing is going on, believe that we have a God of miracles who loves us and wants the best for us. God can "make a way out of no way." I saw Him do it with me, you, and so many others through history! You never know who's got God-given yeast in them waiting to rise. The yeast God puts in us is like *hidden treasures in your field*.

"People will come from the east, west, north, and south. They will sit down at the table in God's kingdom. People who have the lowest place in life now will have the highest place in God's kingdom. And people who have the highest place now will have the lowest place in God's kingdom" (Luke 13:29–30).

(LP) Finish Well

God has a way of making all things equal. That's what makes Him the great I AM. Never take your eye off the prize and always strive to do kingdom work because it has benefits that no one on this earth could possibly reward you for.

Also, our team spirit helps those that are in a low place go high!

There is a story about someone doing just that in the 2016 Summer Olympics in Rio.

New Zealand runner Nikki Hamblin was lying on the track, dazed after a heavy fall and with her hopes of an Olympic medal seemingly over. Suddenly, there was a hand on her shoulder and a voice in her ear: "Get up. We have to finish this." It was American Abbey D'Agostino, offering to help. It was a scene to warm the hearts of fans during a qualifying heat of the women's 5000 meters. Hamblin and D'Agostino set aside their own hopes of making the final to look out for a fellow competitor.

Here is part of a teaching by Pastor Steven J. Cole that I thought would assist us in *finish well:*

Starting that new diet or exercise program is kind of fun, but hanging in over the long haul is the real test. Getting married is exciting and relatively easy. Staying married through the struggles, adjustments, and trials is not always as easy.

The same is true of the Christian life. Becoming a Christian is relatively easy: Acknowledge to God that you are a sinner and receive by faith the free gift of eternal life that Christ provided by His shed blood. But then comes the hard part—hanging in there as a Christian in a world that is hostile toward God and His people. The world constantly dangles in front of you all that it has to offer in opposition to the things of God. From within, the flesh entices you to forsake Christ and gratify your sinful desires. The enemy hits you with temptation after temptation. The real test of your faith is, will you endure? Genuine faith in Christ perseveres to the finish line.

This means that to *finish well*, you need to view all your life as an act of sacrificial worship to God. As Paul put it in Romans 12:1, "Therefore I urge you, brethren, by the mercies of God, to present your bodies a living and holy sacrifice, acceptable to God, which is your spiritual service of worship."

> "Jesus said to them, 'Go tell that fox, 'Today and tomorrow I am forcing demons out of people and finishing my work of healing. Then, the next day, the work will be finished.' After that I must go, because all prophets should die in Jerusalem" (Luke 13:32–33).

(LP) Die Empty

What a sense of accomplishment to know when your work is done—and to already have in place an exit strategy. Wow! In nowadays terms, that would be like a will or life insurance. It allows those who have to make your final arrangements to have less stress in figuring out where they're going to get the money to properly put you to rest.

But the more important thing is that we will leave here knowing in our last breath that the work God gave you to do was truly completed. Another point is that, Jesus himself died at thirty-three—which was young, especially in the lifespan of that era. I can't even speculate about why God would take a child at an early age. Even when we get old and have lived what we consider a full life, we still never want to see anyone go, except in an extreme case of pain and suffering. But to *die empty*, like Bernice King says, "Is a life fulfilled." That's a *hidden treasure*.

Luke 14

*A man with a bad disease was there in front of him.
Jesus said to the Pharisees and experts in the law, "Is
it right or wrong to heal on the Sabbath day?" But
they would not answer his question. So he took the
man and healed him. Then he sent the man away.
Jesus said to the Pharisees and teachers of the law,
"If your son or work animal falls into a well on the
Sabbath day, you know you would pull him out
immediately." The Pharisees and teachers of the law
could say nothing against what he said.*

—Luke 14:2–6

(LP) Lord of the Sabbath

In the movie *Hacksaw Ridge*, there is a Seventh Day Adventist who
joins the military to serve his country. The question came up if he
would participate in the war conflict on the Sabbath day. Technically,
he said no, but when the last day of the conflict fell on the Sabbath
day, he did take some time to pray but joined his fellow comrades
and helped win the war.

I think for everyone, there is a line in the sand. One, is the
importance of following the law. But like Jesus, when someone is in
need, there is another consideration to consider. Even though the
Sabbath is put aside as a holy day, most pastors still have to work.
I believe that decision has to be worked out on an individual basis.

I do believe that a spiritual person should take at least one in
seven days to rest and reflect. Not as a guilt trip, but a true day to
thank our precious Savior for the other six days. Us pastors, generally

take Monday as the day of rest. And every secretary knows not to call the pastor on a Monday, unless it is an extreme emergency. Jesus even mentions that the Sabbath was made for man, not man for the Sabbath and that man is the *Lord of the Sabbath*. One of the *hidden treasures* of this passage is that the needs of mankind should always outweigh a religious observance.

> "So when someone invites you, go sit in the seat that is not important. Then they will come to you and say, 'Friend, move up here to this better place!' What an honor this will be for you in front of all the other guests. Everyone who makes themselves important will be made humble. But everyone who makes themselves humble will be made important" (Luke 14:10–11).

(LP) Humor: A Reflection of God's Love

In days past, when someone choose a career in comedy, it was a very humble and low road to be on. With only a few truly being recognized in the industry. But in this new era, they are being lifted up to have a great career, like we've never seen before.

When I first started bringing humor into my concerts in the eighties. It was a scary proposition, because of the serious nature of Scripture. But the more I would tell truthful and self-debasing stories about my life and a few characters in the Bible. The more I would get invited into traditionally known circles. The stories take folks on a journey through their own failures and missteps and cause them to see God's love from a different vantage point.

Going low will always take you high, no matter if it's popular or not.

As I mentioned before about Pastor Wayne from New Hope Hawaii. Well, he has a sister church in Las Vegas called New Hope of Las Vegas led by Pastor Kent and Lisa Miyoshi. They have been great friends since 2011, and when I'm off tour, we really enjoy the solid messages and the warm and friendly aloha spirit of the people. Plus

Pastor Kent always delivers his message in a funny package, which makes it easier to digest a much-needed spiritual truth. Something along these lines:

How I learned how to mind my own business:

I was walking along the sidewalk next to the mental hospital last week, and all of the patients were chanting, "Thirteen...thirteen... thirteen...thirteen."

The fence was too high to see over the top to find out what they were chanting about, so I looked for another way to see in. I spotted a knot hole and walked over to see for myself. The knot hole was just about eye level, so I leaned into it for a peek. That's when I got poked in the eye with a stick.

And then the chanting continued, "Fourteen...fourteen... fourteen...fourteen..."

Norman Cousins was a longtime editor of the *Saturday Review*, global peacemaker, receiver of hundreds of awards including the UN Peace Medal and nearly fifty honorary doctorate degrees. In 1964 following a very stressful trip to Russia, he was diagnosed with ankylosing spondylitis (a degenerative disease causing the breakdown of collagen), which left him in constant pain, and even his doctor announced he would die within a few months. He disagreed and reasoned that if stress had somehow contributed to his illness, then positive emotions should help him feel better. With his doctors' consent, he checked himself out of the hospital and into a hotel across the street and began taking extremely high doses of vitamin C while exposing himself to a continuous stream of humorous films. He later claimed that ten minutes of belly rippling laughter would give him two hours of pain-free sleep, when nothing else, not even morphine, could help him. His condition steadily improved, and he slowly regained the use of his limbs. Within six months, he was back on his feet, and within two years, he was able to return to his full-time job at the *Saturday Review*. His story baffled the scientific community and inspired a number of research projects.

A man walked to the top of a hill to talk to God. The man asked, "God, what's a million years to you?" and God said, "A minute." Then the man asked, "Well, what's a million dollars to you?"

and God said, "A penny." Then the man asked, "God, can I have a penny?" and God said, "Sure, in a minute."

I believe God uses a lot of different and even unconventional ways to *reflect His love* and well-being for us. Humor is an excellent choice and a *hidden treasure*.

> *Then Jesus said to the Pharisee who had invited him, "When you give a lunch or a dinner, don't invite only your friends, brothers, relatives, and rich neighbors. At another time they will pay you back by inviting you to eat with them. Instead, when you give a feast, invite the poor, the crippled, and the blind. Then you will have great blessings, because these people cannot pay you back. They have nothing. But God will reward you at the time when all godly people rise from death." (Luke 14:12–14)*

(LP) Fringe Benefits

This really begs the question—do you really love your neighbor as yourself or do you love the neighbor that is in your same class or ethnicity? As we continue through this life, we should always make a way for those who would not be able to go to that dinner or movie or school or job site without your help. It is the most rewarding feeling of all because somebody reached out and continues to reach out to us along this life road.

I've been going to visit the men in prison since the middle of the seventies. I knew when I made my conversion in '74 that it was God's heart to do so. The guys are always so excited with the visit. They get inspired by the stories I tell concerning my conversion and life experiences. And with each visit, they seem to be falling more and more in love with our Savior.

I remember one time when I was playing at Disney World in Florida. I was just coming off stage to greet some fans; and a guy in the back started yelling, "Hey, Leon, remember me?" Of course, I meet so many people that it can be the casualty of my profession, not remembering everyone. But when he got closer, he reminded me of the time I visited a facility in Tehachapi, California. He went on to say that he got saved that day when I visited. Then he turned around and introduced me to his children and newly converted wife. It was a fortunate thing for me to see on this side of heaven. A life touched, changed, and experiencing a family reunion. This is one of the *fringe benefits* that comes with this calling—to see God transform a life.

And as a reminder, every reward doesn't come this side of life. God in His mercy has much greater rewards when we join Him later. It always cracks me up that He would reward us with anything. After all, the Cross was the greatest gift that anyone of us could receive! And then there are *fringe benefits* too? Wow! What *hidden treasure*.

> "Jesus said to him, 'A man gave a big dinner. He invited many people. When it was time to eat, he sent his servant to tell the guests, "Come. The food is ready." But all the guests said they could not come. Each one made an excuse'" (Luke 14:16–18).

(LP) Go

Boy, do I hear that a lot. Some people feel it's a waste of time and want to put off their commitment to Him to a much later date. So the Lord prepares the heart of us missionaries for the possibility that people will make excuses. So the idea for us believers is to get the word out to as many as we are physically able. It's our part of the deal to remind ourselves that "It's a joy, Lord, first, that you would entrust such a great honor and responsibility to us. And it shows that you believe, Lord, that with your help, guidance, anointing, and tenacity, that we will be successful in the task. I'm up to it Lord—*send me*! I will pour out my *hidden treasures* for the world to see!"

> "If you wanted to build a building, you would first sit down and decide how much it would cost. You must see if you have enough money to

finish the job. If you don't do that, you might begin the work, but you would not be able to finish. And if you could not finish it, everyone would laugh at you. They would say, 'This man began to build, but he was not able to finish'" (Luke 14:28–30).

(LP) Faith Works

Right off the cuff, it seems like this scripture is telling us, don't have faith. But according to James, it's like, let's see your faith with your deeds.

> Do you want evidence that faith without deeds is useless? Was not our father Abraham considered righteous for what he did when he offered his son Isaac on the altar? You see that his faith and his actions were working together, and his faith was made complete by what he did. And the scripture was fulfilled that says, "Abraham believed God, and it was credited to him as righteousness," and he was called God's friend. You see that a person is considered righteous by what they do and not by faith alone. In the same way, was not even Rahab the prostitute considered righteous for what she did when she gave lodging to the spies and sent them off in a different direction? As the body without the spirit is dead, so faith without deeds is dead. (James 2:20–26, NIV)

I love the practicality of our Lord. We should have a plan and backing for what we are trying to accomplish. This is a big question for me today because I tend to act first, then count the cost later. It has worked in some cases, but I do notice that it makes everything run a little thin, especially if it goes on for years and years in that direction. In times past, it seemed to be the only way to get something done, but as I look at our precious Savior, he had at least twelve dedicated people with Him at all time.

The question we have to ask is this: Is my business plan well spelled out? Can the board members see the vision, and if they do, is there enough funds between us to accomplish the outreach? I want these kids of ours to have a new lyrical content to digest into their system, something that will counteract the onslaught from the dark side. I want my songs to be like glasses that all songs are screened through. I would also pray that their parents and grandparents who have been away from church will return and take up their rightful place as the recipients of great wisdom.

And help me, Lord, to get the backing first, then release the project. I know you are in it, Lord. It's the timing I'm asking for today. And in your perfect timing, this *hidden treasure* will be uncovered. As it continues. "If a king is going to fight against another king, first he will sit down and plan. If he has only 10,000 men, he will try to decide if he is able to defeat the other king who has 20,000 men. If he thinks he cannot defeat the other king, he will send some men to ask for peace while that king's army is still far away" (Luke 14:31–32).

(LP) Simple Negotiation Will Set You Free

See, another angle on the same theme. No sooner did I ask, then an answer came. Another thought too that we all run into is this: What if you do see yourself not being able to be timely with your financial obligation, what should you do? My answer would be, at the least call and make your creditors aware of your dilemma and work out a payment plan that you feel you can accomplish. It shows *integrity* and puts your Christian witness way up on top of the hill. It also shows that you're not running from your responsibility, and believe it or not, you will feel a sense of peace in the middle of the storm! *Negotiating* bills is *hidden treasures in your field.* Everybody has some level of communication to negotiate. Even if you're frightened to death about the possibility of a negative outcome from your plea, a few of your creditors or business associates or even boss will have an ear to hear and it will at first shock you. But it will help to restore your faith in God's ability to reach their hearts and will help restore your faith in humanity again.

A man's favorite donkey falls into a deep precipice. He can't pull it out no matter how hard he tries. He therefore decides to bury it alive. Soil is poured onto the donkey from above. The donkey feels the load, shakes it off, and steps on it. More soil is poured. It shakes it off and steps up. The more the load was poured, the higher the donkey rose. By noon the donkey had walked right out of the pit and was grazing in green pastures. I say to you today, after much shaking off and stepping up, one day you will be grazing in green pastures.

A lot of our fear comes from bad past experiences, but the Bible says we should keep asking, keep seeking, keep knocking, and the door will be opened.

A man was passing some elephants outside a circus area. He suddenly stopped, confused by the fact that these huge creatures were being held by only a small rope tied to their front leg. No chains, no cages. It was obvious that the elephants could, at any time, break away from their bonds; but for some reason, they didn't.

The man asked the trainer nearby why these animals just stood there and made no attempt to get away. "Well," the trainer said, "when they are very young and much smaller, we used the same-sized rope to tie them and at that age it was enough to hold them. Even though they are grown-up, they have become conditioned to the bondage. So they still believe the rope can hold them...and they never try to break free."

These animals could break free from their bonds at any time, but because they believed they couldn't, they stay right where they are. Like the elephants, how many of us go through life hanging on to a belief that we cannot do something, simply because of some bondage or failure from the past. God should be our first *negotiation* point—and *freedom* will follow.

> "It is the same for each of you. You must leave everything you have to follow me. If not, you cannot be my follower" (Luke 14:33).

(LP) Personal

So one must pour everything into the task at hand—no short-cuts or excuses make it the best. This so encourages me with my music and lyrical reach. I want it to be set apart from everyone else. I will go around the pack and set up a new music genre that the rest will follow. It would be a travesty if all groups, Grammy-award shows academy and alike, don't include this music style somewhere in its programming. Amen!

> "Salt is a good thing. But if the salt loses its salty taste, you can't make it salty again. It is worth nothing. You can't even use it as dirt or dung. People just throw it away. 'You people who hear me, listen!'" (Luke 14:34–35).

(LP) Personal Note: "Don't Lose Your Influence"

Keep the flavor of who you are and what you represent. It will be a surprise to all when they see you busting forth out of the dust. *"Nations as your inheritance, world as your possession."* Keep going. Jesus is about to set you free to that which you have been called to be, now and into eternity. Walk as if king. Feel as if servant. Move as unafraid. Sing as if it's the antioxidant songs for our nation. Don't back down, but go forward with more passion than ever before.

A note: This book was originally formed to inject scripture into my heart. So I'm leaving a few of these personal words of encouragement in so you, my friend, can see into the back door of my heart.

I remember the first time I played at Disney World. I had to enter through the employee's entrance. It wasn't as glamorous as coming through the front gate. But I got to see the working mechanism of what made the park so phenomenal. I hope the personal things I share will have the same effect on you and gives you another view of our blessed and creative Savior. And there will be more of these personal notes in and through this book.

Luke 15

Then the Pharisees and the teachers of the law began to complain, "Look, this man welcomes sinners and even eats with them!" Then Jesus told them this story: "Suppose one of you has 100 sheep, but one of them gets lost. What will you do? You will leave the other 99 sheep there in the field and go out and look for the lost sheep. You will continue to search for it until you find it. And when you find it, you will be very happy. You will carry it home, go to your friends and neighbors and say to them, 'Be happy with me because I found my lost sheep!' In the same way, I tell you, heaven is a happy place when one sinner decides to change. There is more joy for that one sinner than for 99 good people who don't need to change."

—Luke 15:2–7

(LP) One Is More Than a Hundred

A lot of us make our living taking care of sheep, which is a noble and much-needed calling. And some of us go after lost people just like someone came after us. And sometimes we don't want to get our hands dirty by dealing with all the foul language and words of rejection and ridicule. I know it was uncomfortable for Richard to approach me every time I came to visit his sister especially when spirituality was the last thing on my mind in those days. But he was persistent, and millions of lives have been altered because of it.

All it takes is *one* to become convinced of the claims of Christ, and the domino effect is put into place. Not only is that person saved and comforted through all life's living, but everywhere that person goes, if he or she is influential or not, seeds of the Kingdom are being planted.

That's the motivation and the philosophy behind the *Ready 2 Rise* CD. To go after the *one* that would have an ear to hear. Like the voices that spoke into our generation, may God continue to remind us of the joy that *one* brings to His heart, oppose to the ninety-nine good people who don't need to change. What a *hidden treasure*. And it continues: "Suppose a woman has ten silver coins, but she loses one of them. She will take a light and clean the house. She will look carefully for the coin until she finds it. And when she finds it, she will call her friends and neighbors and say to them, "Be happy with me because I have found the coin that I lost!" In the same way, it's a happy time for the angels of God when one sinner decides to change."

(LP) Keep Stretching

I love the word *change* used by the ERV version. It reminds us that at any point in our lives, we can change. To me it means to make new patterns to live by when we are being trapped by a repetitive cycle. It's like the Israelites who went around and around in the desert. You feel like you're going somewhere, but you keep seeing the same scenery. Continue to push, my friend, toward the straight line. Eventually the landscape will change, and the lights from your promised land will shine brighter and brighter.

I know the Lord may not be speaking about this subject matter specifically, but it popped into my head that this scripture could be motivational for a career change or a new and higher influencing position, especially for someone like me who has been there and done that and suddenly feels a push to go at it again. One has to pull from a different incentive, especially when you get to a certain maturity in life.

I intercede for all of us who need just that little something to get going again. For me, it's the kids. When I'm investigating their songs and checking tempos and such, one, I feel so old and the other emotion is, challenged to not be outdone. I'm very competitive. It's exhausting to tell you the truth, so I have to keep going to scripture to make sure this is God's will and not just some whim.

Give me ears to hear, Lord…and let me see through your eyes and feel with your heart.

Personal:

Well, I got an answer today, like when I first got saved. I would ask and out would come the answer! Well, *I'm back*! We drove to Lola's house (Renee's mom) because she was having a hard time breathing, and she had and has had a few heart attacks. After spending some time discussing her five wishes, I knew I had to step up in helps and in dollars. This is the spark I needed to invite overwhelming success to my door. And *doggone it, I will succeed*. The whole idea behind *treasures* is so that we can share them!

So the father divided his wealth between his two sons.

A few days later the younger son gathered up all that he had and left. He traveled far away to another country, and there he wasted his money living like a fool. After he spent everything he had, there was a terrible famine throughout the country. He was hungry and needed money. So he went and got a job with one of the people who lived there. The man sent him into the fields to feed pigs. He was so hungry that he wanted to eat the food the pigs were eating. But no one gave him anything.

The son realized that he had been very foolish. He thought, "All my father's hired workers have plenty of food. But here I am, almost dead because I have nothing to eat. I will leave and go to my father. I will say to him: 'Father, I have

sinned against God and have done wrong to you.
I am no longer worthy to be called your son. But
let me be like one of your hired workers.'" So he
left and went to his father. (Luke 15:13–20)

(LP) Foolish, Disaster, Desperation, Transformation

When we depart from the path, it's a *foolish move*. Then *disaster* hits. *Desperation* follows, and somewhere in that last stage, *transformation comes*. This was the pattern of the wayward son. I think all of us do foolish things—even after we get saved. In fact, I hear the super rich mention this in our conferences. They say, "We have so much money and things, that we're bored."

This may not be the case for everyone, but a great percentage choose different things to medicate themselves with. Some, even physicians and psychiatrist, commit suicide as a remedy. So once you've done a *foolish* thing, the normal repercussion is *disaster*.

Like the prodigal son, when he got desperate for money, he took a job—not only feeding pigs but desiring their food. In his moment of desperation, he started to think and most likely pray. Then it came to him, a way out of his mess! Go home! He even practiced his speech on the way. The one thing I do like about his approach to his dad was humility. He admitted he was wrong and declared himself unworthy of his father's love. But this is where the parallel of the Lord comes in. The father didn't condemn him after his statement of confession. He rewarded him with gifts and blessings and a social event to announce the homecoming of his son, as if he had been off to war and came through it successfully.

Truly this was a relief for the son, and in a sense, he was in a war—the age-old battle between good and evil. *Transformation* comes as a result of what one has been through.

Once upon a time a daughter complained to her father that her life was miserable and that she didn't know how she was going to make it. She was tired of fighting and struggling all the time. It seemed just as one problem was solved, another one soon followed. Her father, a chef, took her to the kitchen. He filled three pots with water and placed each on a high fire. Once the three pots began to boil, he placed potatoes in one pot, eggs in the second pot, and ground coffee beans in the third pot. After twenty minutes he turned off the burners. He took the potatoes out of the pot and placed them in a bowl. He pulled the eggs out and placed them in a bowl. He then took the coffee out and placed it in a cup. "Father, what does this mean?" she asked.

He then explained that the potatoes, the eggs, and coffee beans had each faced the same adversity, the boiling water. However, each one reacted differently.

The potato went in strong, hard, and unrelenting; but in boiling water, it became soft and weak. The egg was fragile, with the thin outer shell protecting its liquid interior, until it was put in the boiling water. Then the inside of the egg became hard. However, the ground coffee beans were unique. After they were exposed to the boiling water, they changed the water and created something new.

"When adversity knocks on your door, how do you respond? Are you a potato, an egg, or a coffee bean?" In life, things happen around us, things happen to us, but the only thing that truly matters is what happens within us to cause a true *transformation*!

> The older son was angry and would not go into the party. So his father went out and begged him to come in. But he said to his father, "Look, for all these years I have worked like a slave for you. I have always done what you told me to do, and you never gave me even a young goat for a party with my friends. But then this son of yours comes home after wasting your money on prostitutes, and you kill the best calf for him!"
>
> His father said to him, "Oh, my son, you are always with me, and everything I have is yours. But this was a day to be happy and celebrate. Your brother was dead, but now he is alive. He was lost, but now he is found." (Luke 15:28–32)

(LP) Undeserved Mercy

First, it's good to realize that the father in his wisdom had established individual relationships with each child. And he dealt with each according to their personalities and gifts. This is an eye-opener, just in that. But it must have been hard for the Dad to receive criticism from the older brother, after all he had consistently done for him.

Another point I get out of this is that the older son only saw how much money had been spent and didn't even recognize the defeat the younger son had over the demons in his life. The father always desires us to ask for forgiveness humbly and with a contrite and remorseful heart. That's the start. Then day by day work through the issues that bring one to that place of peace. And with the guidance of the Holy Spirit and possibly some counseling, any one of us can have a breakthrough. It's a consistent trait of our Lord to give us *undeserved mercy*, but it turns out to be *hidden treasures in our field*.

Luke 16

"How much do you owe my master?" He answered, "I owe him 100 jars of olive oil." The manager said to him, "Here is your bill. Hurry! Sit down and make the bill less. Write 50 jars." Then the manager asked another one, "How much do you owe my master?" He answered, "I owe him 100 measures of wheat." Then the manager said to him, "Here is your bill; you can make it less. Write 80 measures." Later, the master told the dishonest manager that he had done a smart thing. Yes, worldly people are smarter in their business with each other than spiritual people are. I tell you, use the worldly things you have now to make "friends" for later. Then, when those things are gone, you will be welcomed into a home that lasts forever.

—Luke 16:5–9

(LP) Personal Note: Pep Talk

I feel a direct connection to this servant. I need to up my game and boldly step into the big arena. So many ways, the Lord has communicated with me about this next move and I need to continue preparing and repairing my heart, my body, and my soul. Besides my music, let me take a stab at it from another angle today, Lord. And may the outcome be positive, affirming, prophetic, and encouraging.

It's okay to talk to yourself like this. I have heard over and over through the years that King David had to command his soul to praise the Lord. Even if you're walking down a busy street with people everywhere, just put your cell phone up to you head and start encouraging yourself. Side note: Make sure you turn the ringer off.

You'll be surprised how refreshed you will feel when you arrive at your destination. How sure-footed you will feel, even at the checkout counter of a store, where you might not smile so much. But because of a *pep talk*, you're smiling and saying hello to perfect strangers.

This book was written for us to share. It embodies *hidden treasures*, which, when they are revealed, will alter us in much-needed areas. May we shed the old layer of dead, unproductive skin and let new life begin to emerge fresh and new again. Jesus even encourages it. He calls it returning to your first love, which is the ultimate *hidden treasure.*

The verse above that has always baffled me was verse 9, "I tell you, use the worldly things you have now to make 'friends' for later. Then, when those things are gone, you will be welcomed into a home that lasts forever."

I'll give you my take on this, which may run parallel to something similar in your life. For instance, contemporary Christian music has shifted considerably. In times past, us pioneers have been praying for more workers in the field but now the market is saturated! So as I have stated before, people have to find ways to reinvent themselves to remain relevant.

I know that the scripture above is making a reference in the last part to our eternal home. But putting it into terms this side of heaven, it simply means to continue working on that gift or thing that makes you valuable. And when everyone else gives up, gets tired, and drops out, your light of consistency will stand out from everyone else. And because of that, you will be welcomed into an influential circle of people, even in your retirement years. Good one, huh?

Here are just a few examples: Michael Jordan has continued to enterprise with Hanes. Cell phone companies keep pushing the technology envelop to give us more and more features. Arnold Palmer and Jimmy Dean continued their legacy through foods and drinks. When it says in verse 8, "Worldly people are smarter in their business with each other than spiritual people are," it's trying to tell us that we have to work extra hard to keep the world looking in our direction, admiring us so much so that they will have to engage us in some way. I hope you will be able to capitalize on this little extra *hidden treasure*.

A popular speaker started off a seminar by holding up a $20 bill. A crowd of two hundred had gathered to hear him speak. He asked, "Who would like this $20 bill?" Two hundred hands went up. He said, "I am going to give this $20 to one of you, but first, let me do this." He crumpled the bill up. He then asked, "Who still wants it?" All two hundred hands were still raised. "Well," he replied, "what if I do this?" Then he dropped the bill on the ground and stomped on it with his shoes. He picked it up and showed it to the crowd. The bill was all crumpled and dirty. "Now who still wants it?" All the hands still went up.

"My friends, I have just showed you a very important lesson. No matter what I did to the money, you still wanted it because it did not decrease in value. It was still worth $20. Many times in our lives life crumples us and grinds us into the dirt. We make bad decisions or deal with poor circumstances. We feel worthless. But no matter what has happened or what will happen, you will never lose your value. You are special, don't ever forget it!

> "The Pharisees were listening to all these things. They criticized Jesus because they all loved money. Jesus said to them, 'You make yourselves look good in front of people. But God knows what is really in your hearts. What people think is important is worth nothing to God'" (Luke 16:14–15).

(LP) What People Think Is Important Is Worth Nothing to God

This should really lift your spirit today like it's doing to mine. "What people think is important is worth nothing to God." Wow!

From time to time I watch movies and hear songs that are like eating cardboard—chomping down on something that doesn't satisfy and definitely not nutritional. But when we hear the announcers hype or watch compelling commercials, it makes us feel like it's the greatest thing since sliced bread.

I think that's why scripture has been so important for the Christian. We too can get caught up in the hoopla if we don't have a standard to live by.

In Revelations 3:15–16, it says, "I know your deeds, that you are neither cold nor hot. I wish you were either one or the other! So, because you are lukewarm—neither hot nor cold—I am about to spit you out of my mouth."

I took a pastor friend to a movie, during one of our off days, to try and give him some laughter. We went to a movie that was really not my first choice, language wise. Of course, it was funny because we both came out of the same culture the movie was set in. But when we got back to the car, I had to apologize for some of the language. I wish I had just got up and walked out, like I have, on some other films. But to my shame, I didn't. One thing it has made me do is to investigate other movies fully before I take someone or suggest that they go see it.

"What people think is important is worth nothing to God." The *hidden treasure* of a classy Christian!

> The rich man said, "Then please, father Abraham, send Lazarus to my father's house on earth. I have five brothers. He could warn my brothers so that they will not come to this place of pain."
>
> But Abraham said, "They have the Law of Moses and the writings of the prophets to read; let them learn from that."
>
> The rich man said, "No, father Abraham! But if someone came to them from the dead, then they would decide to change their lives."
>
> But Abraham said to him, "If your brothers won't listen to Moses and the prophets, they won't listen to someone who comes back from the dead." (Luke 16:27–31)

(LP) No Atheist in the Foxholes

Wow, how true is that scripture, in light of the fact that Jesus rose from the dead two thousand years ago! With historic evidence to prove it, and people are still trippin! But as I always say, people that battle a deadly disease or a near-death experience get a different view of their life beyond this one. Sometimes it takes one of those near-death experiences to wake us up, like 911.

It's also good to note how much respect Lazarus, all of a sudden, was getting from the rich man. He didn't even give him the time of day on earth, now he doesn't mind if he goes to his closest family member's house. I don't wish this on anyone, but disaster can put a lot of things in perspective!

A quick story: I remember when our motorhome caught on fire. We had just finished a concert in Northern California where we transported not only the band, but their wives too. At the end of the weekend, we dropped everyone off and Renee and I started heading back to Vegas. The I-15 was so jammed with traffic that we decided to go the back way past Laughlin. As soon as we turned on to the new highway, Renee yelled, "Smoke!" I looked up, and the ceiling air conditioner was on fire. Being that the rig was mostly flammable, the fire and smoke spread quickly.

I had time to pull over, but the fire had burnt through the electric switches that triggered the doors and windows. I couldn't see Renee because she was over by the kitchen midway the coach. But I could hear her yelling, "Jesus, Jesus," and kicking the door. I, on the other hand, just before the fire, had rolled down my window a slight bit. It was open just enough for me to squeeze through and jump face first to the ground.

Just as I was going around toward Renee's door, it suddenly flew open with her running out and coughing. I took her by the hand and started running away from the motorhome that was billowing smoke because we had just filled up with gas and propane. And just like out of a movie scene, it exploded as fire shot into the air.

A ways away, we were standing there watching, with no shoes and no coats, watching our ride and some of our possessions go up in smoke. Then a truck with a God-hearted man stopped on the road and asked if we were all right. We said yes, and we thanked him for stopping to check on us. Then he said, "I'll be right back," and returned with two pair of shoes for us. And praise God, he and his girlfriend had the exact same size shoe as us.

The story became national news and is still trending online. The blessing was that, we had just paid cash for this rig on Friday and Renee begged me to get it insured. I fought with her over that issue because we were on a time restraint to pick up the band. But in the end, she prevailed. Thank God she did because the motorhome had melted to the ground by Monday. The weird thing was the fire happened on October 31. It was a real life attack to try and take us out! But Jesus had our backs on this one.

This almost tragic event was eye-opening in many ways. We were alive and very thankful for that. But this encounter brought us closer than ever in our relationship. The money, checks, stage instruments, street clothes, Renee's wedding ring, and a lot of items that were dear to us, were all gone in a flash. This showed us not to put too much value in possessions. So when I hear a lot of people on the tube or social media talking down my Savior, I say to myself, you just haven't been faced with a real tragedy yet, one that would let you know that if it wasn't for the grace of God, you'd be out of here. Like I tell most skeptics, Benny Hinn can look controversial or even comical to a person full of health. But get sick, and you'll find yourself sliding toward the TV and putting your hands on it for a healing!

Jesus, the only one in recorded history that ever rose from the dead, He is truly the resurrection and the life, a true *hidden treasure*!

Luke 17

Jesus said to his followers, "Things will surely happen that will make people sin. But it will be very bad for anyone who makes this happen. It will be very bad for anyone who makes one of these little children sin. It would be better for them to have a millstone tied around their neck and be drowned in the sea. So be careful!"

—Luke 17:1–3

(LP) Suffer the Little Children

So again, a reference to children and their preciousness to our Lord. Make me mindful of all that I need to do, Lord, to accommodate your heart.

A mother and a baby camel were lying around under a tree. Then the baby camel asked, "Why do camels have humps?" The mother camel considered this and said, "We are desert animals so we have the humps to store water so we can survive with very little water." The baby camel thought for a moment then said, "Okay, why are our legs long and our feet rounded?" The mama replied, "They are meant for walking in the desert." The baby paused. After a beat, the camel asked, "Why are our eyelashes long? Sometimes they get in my way." The mama responded, "Those long thick eyelashes protect your eyes from the desert sand when it blows in the wind."

The baby thought and thought. Then he said, "I see. So the hump is to store water when we are in the desert, the legs are for walking through the desert, and these eyelashes protect my eyes from the desert, then what are were doing in the zoo?"

Kids are so special, no matter what species they are.

> "The apostles said to the Lord, 'Give us more
> faith!' The Lord said, 'If your faith is as big as a
> mustard seed, you can say to this mulberry tree,
> "Dig yourself up and plant yourself in the ocean!"
> And the tree will obey you'" (Luke 17:5–6).

(LP) How Big Is Your Faith?

Wow, really? I've seen miracles in my day, but I fall short in even having a mustard seed of faith, which I have heard is the smallest little thing. As I mentioned before, Pastor Mel in St. Louis, Missouri, and I had a discussion about miracles happen for people in remote places. He said it's because they have no...other...options. In the case of those of us who live in areas of choice, we have so many options for healing. Many don't need to believe at that level.

That's why I like ministering in places where there is a celebration when I come. Yuba City, for instance, is a perfect example of a spot like that; or Wentzville, Missouri; or Australia; or the Midwest; or East Coast. Hmm, that's just about everywhere, huh?

When Jesus touches people in their most needy places, it's like watching a diamond form out of coal or a pearl out of an oyster. I come to bless them, but every time I walk away shaking my head in amazement at their bigger-than-mustard-seed faith—a *hidden treasure*.

> They all had leprosy. But the men shouted,
> "Jesus! Master! Please help us!"
> When Jesus saw the men, he said, "Go and
> show yourselves to the priests."
> While the ten men were going to the priests,
> they were healed. When one of them saw that
> he was healed, he went back to Jesus. He praised
> God loudly. He bowed down at Jesus' feet and
> thanked him. (He was a Samaritan.) Jesus said,

"Ten men were healed; where are the other nine? This man is not even one of our people. Is he the only one who came back to give praise to God?" Then Jesus said to the man, "Stand up! You can go. You were healed because you believed." (Luke 17:13–19)

(LP) Give Thanks to the Lord for He Is Good

During the beginning stages of the Jesus Movement, I was a participant, not realizing that history was being made. Like the Samaritan, a lot of us secular musicians were being saved and reassigned. It took the traditional church by surprise, but it was truly a God thing. Like the Samaritan, we were shouting and praising God loudly with our voices and instruments. Unashamed of proclaiming the name of Jesus in a nonreligious environment. And some said the same thing about us, that there is no way they can be a part of the body of Christ. It must be some sort of occult. But the music and its message have stood the test of time.

I and many others still receive correspondence about how our fans' children were raised listening to our albums. Also like the Samaritan, we should "give thanks to the Lord, for He is good. His loving kindness is ever lasting." It should be a part of our normal dialogue to always be whispering up words of thanks, and in a more formal setting, we should always express our gratitude to Jesus. I will be mindful of that in my asking and will also do more thanking. A *hidden treasure* for sure.

A twenty-four-year-old boy seeing out from the train's window shouted, "Dad, look the trees are going behind!" Dad smiled, and a young couple sitting nearby, looked at the twenty-four-year-old's childish behavior with pity. Suddenly, he again exclaimed, "Dad, look the clouds are running with us!" The couple couldn't resist and said to the old man, "Why don't you take your son to a good doctor?" The old man smiled and said, "I did, and we are just coming from the hospital. My son was blind from birth, and he just got his eyes today."

It would be nice to be that proud and blurt out our appreciation for God's goodness. Our walk with Jesus should give us something to shout about—every day!

> "Some of the Pharisees asked Jesus, 'When will God's kingdom come?' Jesus answered, "God's kingdom is coming, but not in a way that you can see it. People will not say, 'Look, God's kingdom is here!' or 'There it is!' No, God's kingdom is here with you" (Luke 17:20–21).

(LP) What's There Cannot Always Be Seen

"Not by might, not by power, but by my Spirit," saith the Lord is the first scripture to come to mind. I do realize that you can't see the Spirit, but you can feel it. It's like the air. We know it's there because we feel it brushing pass our face and hair. But this type of sweet awareness takes a minute to develop. That's one of the things that baffle's the scientific community—the fact that it is not measurable on any meter. Maybe God set it up that way because to have something come out of nothing is always a testimony to the unseen world.

Some people claim they can make anything that God has made. Then I say, "Yeah, but do it from scratch without any materials to start with." God's kingdom is a mystery, but we got a little glimpse of the unseen when the word became flesh and dwelt among us. The *hidden treasure* himself.

A lyric from the *Ready 2 Rise* album says, "You make a way out of know way, you make a way out of none. You make a thing that's impossible, come right out of the power of, your tongue."

We can't see gravity, yet it has a profound effect on our lives. It is so profound that we don't ever really think about it. It gives us a down and an up—that is clear. It orients us in our environment. It makes all the floating and flying objects appear divine. Even a balloon can capture our joy because it rises effortlessly. Birds are considered free because they can escape gravity. It gives us something to push against. It gives us the bottom, a place where we can't fall any farther.

We can't see love. It is a force that changes our lives. We can see the effects of love. We can see the particulars of it: the presents, the touch, the actions. But we cannot see the actual thing referred to as love. It is invisible. And yet babies understand it. They need it to live. We all do, but it is still not a thing that we can put in a drawer and save for later.

We can't see the past, yet it is something that sometimes dominates our present lives. We are often living in the past, though we still can't see it. We are convinced that the past is a place that we could visit, if only we had the right time machine.

We can't see radio waves. We can't see sound waves. We can't see ultraviolet waves. We can't see so many vibrations on the spectrum. We can't see the wireless signals that carry the information for the Internet or the voices for our phone calls, but yet the activity from it is present.

We can't see God, but many of us are committed to his existence.

I could go on and on for the whole rest of this book. But you get the point. *What's there cannot always be seen.*

> "Whoever tries to keep the life they have will lose it. But whoever gives up their life will save it. That night there may be two people sleeping in one room. One will be taken and the other will be left. There may be two women working together. One will be taken and the other will be left."
>
> The followers asked Jesus, "Where will this be, Lord?"
>
> Jesus answered, "It's like looking for a dead body—you will find it where the vultures are gathering above." (Luke 17:33–37)

(LP) Live Ready

So like the movie *Left Behind*, it sounds like there will be a lot of chaos—bodies spread out all over the planet. I bet at that time, the credit will go to an alien invasion, which the cinema has been setting us up for, for a long time. Even when I was growing up, although as I look back, the characters weren't as believable as they are now. But the mind-set of aliens of some sort have been consistently planted in our thinking. We can almost envision Thor and the group showing up from one of the nine realms or whatever!

We should *live ready*, as if each day was the day the Lord may show up, working and playing with the Kingdom in our hearts. It's an energizing experience. Then our dependence on the world to supply what it can't gets brought into reality. Sometimes we expect to experience joys this side of heaven as a payback for all our hard work. When the joy, this side of heaven, doesn't even compare with the other side, we should *live in expectation* of something greater because this is not all there is. There is a *treasure hidden* yet to be revealed.

Luke 18

*Then Jesus taught the followers that they should
always pray and never lose hope. He used this story to
teach them: "Once there was a judge in a town. He
did not care about God. He also did not care what
people thought about him. In that same town there
was a woman whose husband had died. She came
many times to this judge and said, 'There is a man
who is doing bad things to me. Give me my rights!'
But the judge did not want to help the woman.
After a long time, the judge thought to himself, 'I
don't care about God. And I don't care about what
people think. But this woman is bothering me. If
I give her what she wants, then she will leave me
alone. But if I don't give her what she wants, she
will bother me until I am sick.'"*

—Luke 18:1–5

(LP) Be Stubborn and Never Give Up!

Some years ago I played out this woman character in a comedic
expression. If you want to find it, it's called, "The Widow" in the
album *A Funny Thing Happened*. I listened to it the other day, and
it's still funny and makes a good point of how the woman never gave
up until the judge gave her justice.

Another teaching point for us believers is that Jesus made a
statement and then followed it with a story. A modern version of
that is Joel Osteen. He catches a group of people on TV that would
never go to a church, synagogue, or a mosque. I have a few Jewish

and Muslim friends who listen to him every Sunday. And I'm glad he is not being swayed away from his call because someone with a membership of fifty is complaining. He has decided to challenge himself to communicate to the unchurched.

So confident am I in my new genre of music that I don't have time to waste on if someone likes it or not. There will be more helped than ever imagined. So be bullheaded like the widow. *Never give up*, and you will eventually get justice. *Being stubborn*, for the right cause, can be a good thing and a *hidden treasure*.

The three Hebrew boys were stubborn and never gave up (paraphrased). The king of that day wanted everyone in the land to bow down to a statue he had made to honor him. But the three did not agree. The king even threatened them, saying he was going to turn up the furnace seven times its heat and throw them in if they didn't bow down to the statue. There comment was a very stubborn comment in favor of their God. They said, "Even if God chooses to not deliver us from the furnace, we will never bow down to your statue." And after many attempts to convince them otherwise, the king had them thrown in. But to his surprise, they never burned up. In fact they were walking around in the fire and some saw an image of Jesus walking around in there with them. The only thing that got burned up that day were the ropes and chains that were binding them, which is another teaching altogether.

Whenever I relive that event, my faith grows a little stronger. It makes me bolder, more tenacious, and more stubborn to accomplish the full expression of my God-given gifting. So, as far as you *stubborn* people, it's not a bad thing after all. Some may just need to be impassioned toward God's purpose.

> The tax collector stood alone too. But when he prayed, he would not even look up to heaven. He felt very humble before God. He said, "O God, have mercy on me. I am a sinner!" I tell you, when this man finished his prayer and went home, he was right with God. But the Pharisee, who felt that he was better than others, was not right with

God. People who make themselves important will
be made humble. But those who make themselves
humble will be made important. (Luke 18:13–14)

(LP) Humble Never Fails

There it is again, humility before God. It goes a long way and
is a daily reminder of a penitent heart. Oh, this is wonderful news!
At least we know we're giving God some pleasure every time we process life in this way. A truly humble person is hard to find, yet God
delights to honor such selfless people.

Booker T. Washington, the renowned black educator, was an
outstanding example of this truth. Shortly after he took over the presidency of Tuskegee Institute in Alabama, he was walking in an exclu-
sive section of town when he was stopped by a wealthy white woman.
Not knowing the famous Mr. Washington by sight, she asked if he
would like to earn a few dollars by chopping wood for her. Because
he had no pressing business at the moment, Professor Washington
smiled, rolled up his sleeves, and proceeded to do the humble chore
she had requested. When he was finished, he carried the logs into the
house and stacked them by the fireplace. A little girl recognized him
and later revealed his identity to the lady.

The next morning the embarrassed woman went to see Mr.
Washington in his office at the Institute and apologized profusely.
"It's perfectly all right, madam," he replied. "Occasionally, I enjoy a
little manual labor. Besides, it's always a delight to do something for
a friend." She shook his hand warmly and assured him that his meek
and gracious attitude had endeared him and his work to her heart.
Not long afterward she showed her admiration by persuading some
wealthy acquaintances to join her in donating thousands of dollars to
the Tuskegee Institute. *Humble never fails!*

Wakefield tells the story of the famous inventor Samuel Morse
who was once asked if he ever encountered situations where he didn't
know what to do. Morse responded, "More than once, and whenever
I could not see my way clearly, I knelt down and prayed to God for
light and understanding."

Morse received many honors from his invention of the telegraph but felt undeserving: "I have made a valuable application of electricity not because I was superior to other men but solely because God, who meant it for mankind, must reveal it to someone and He was pleased to reveal it to me."

I feel the same way about my song, "Flesh of My Flesh." It's still hard to believe that with all the thousands of years before I was born that no one had picked up on what a great love song that Scripture could become. I guess the Lord saw so many couples looking for the right song to accompany their holy union that He gave me that honor—and an honor it truly is. I'm humbled, Lord, that an unworthy vessel like me could be an instrument in the most precious union of all, marriage!

> Some people brought their small children to Jesus so that he could lay his hands on them to bless them. But when the followers saw this, they told the people not to do this. But Jesus called the little children to him and said to his followers, "Let the little children come to me. Don't stop them, because God's kingdom belongs to people who are like these little children. The truth is, you must accept God's kingdom like a little child accepts things, or you will never enter it." (Luke 18:15–17)

(LP) To Be Childlike Is to be Free

This is one of the most powerful scriptures of all. And note that *"the Kingdom belongs to people who are* like *these little children."*

I made a list of how our hearts could respond if we were "people like these little children":

Accept God's kingdom like a little child accepts things: childlike faith, childlike belief in people, childlike smile, childlike adventure to life, childlike simplicity, childlike wonder and imagination, childlike dependence on the guardians in one's life, childlike questions as to why things can't be perfect, childlike belief in his or her gifts, childlike display of no fear or intimidation, childlike faithfulness and intimacy, childlike attitude when standing up for a friend who's being picked on or bullied, childlike wishes and prayers, childlike in not being afraid of life or death, childlike laughter, and childlike tears.

To be childlike is to be free—one of the sweetest aspects of the *hidden treasures*.

I think of Renee's grandmother in the Philippines, who died at 108. She was laughing with her great-grandkids in the backyard, then rolled over and met Jesus. We always hear the phrase, "He died laughing." Well, it literally happened to her. What a way to go—listening to the laughter of little children, then immediately hearing the laughter of kids in heaven. I bet you, it was seamless. Childlikeness, a powerful stress reducer and a *hidden treasure*.

> *Dad*: Do you want Fruit Loops for dinner?
> *Son*: No! That isn't dinner cereal.

> *Question*: What ever happen to Adam and Eve?
> *Little Boy*: God sent them to hell, then transferred them to Los Angeles.

> *Question*: What do you learn from Jesus turning water into wine?
> *Little Girl*: The more wine we get, the better the wedding is.

> *Question*: When God punished Eve, what did He make her become?
> *Little Girl*: A housewife.

> *Question*: Who was George Washington's wife?
> *Little Boy*: Miss America.

To be childlike is to be free!

> A religious leader asked Jesus, "Good Teacher, what must I do to get eternal life?"

Jesus said to him, "Why do you call me good? Only God is good. And you know his commands: 'You must not commit adultery, you must not murder anyone, you must not steal, you must not tell lies about others, you must respect your father and mother.'" (Luke 18:18–19)

(LP) The Big L

Again, this doesn't seem religious. It just sounds like common sense. One of these days we're going to have a rule book like this to be taught in every school throughout the entire world. Maybe then we can interrupt a potential terrorist. Another book title could be *Guide for Kids to Grow By* or *Kids Interactive Guide* or *Love Notes*.

The hunger is there in the kids, that's for sure. I was preparing a bunch of wonderful kids to sing with me at Pastor Jimmy's at Calvary Chapel Lone Mountain. The question came up—"What is the greatest thing we can do with our lives?" I told them that there were two things we can do: love God and love those around us. I call it the *Big L*. I had them sing the song I wrote for them called "My Family" from the *You Can Begin Again* CD. It's a tearjerker for sure, and I had them sing it to their parent in the audience. It's one of those songs I think every kid should learn and sing to their parents.

The reason I call this sort of song the big L is because sometimes the lyrics of a song reflect our love for Jesus and some songs are encouragement to those in the audience, just like "My Family."

I believe the verses give a foundation for all the others to grow from. Our nation and the world is in big trouble right now. There has always been an underlined racial tension that continues to escalate. In Matthew 24:10–12, Jesus says it this way: "At that time many will turn away from the faith and will betray and hate each other, and many false prophets will appear and deceive many people. Because of the increase of wickedness, the love of most will grow cold."

But His advice is this: "But the one who stands firm to the end will be saved. And this gospel of the kingdom will be preached in the whole world as a testimony to all nations, and then the end will come."

Truly the verses above cut to the core of our actions; and if we just follow those "No Adultery," "No Murder," "Don't Steal," "Don't Lie," and respect our parents, the whole next generation could get our nation on track. And we'd have the perfect L—some love going up and some love going out! A perfect *hidden treasure.*

> When the people heard this, they said, "Then who can be saved?"
>
> Jesus answered, "God can do things that are not possible for people to do."
>
> Peter said, "Look, we left everything we had and followed you."
>
> Jesus said, "I can promise that everyone who has left their home, wife, brothers, parents, or children for God's kingdom will get much more than they left. They will get many times more in this life. And in the world that is coming they will get the reward of eternal life." (Luke 18:26–30)

(LP) God Can Do Thee Impossible

What a great reminder when our minds get all caught up in doubt and speculation. One must keep the PURPOSE acrostic in view and keep plowing through. Even when those we trust with our heart commit to the contrary, it's important to our psyche and mental and spiritual health to stay positive because *God can do thee impossible.*

Also, prioritizing *the call* over that which most of us hold precious in our lives, like family, is also a staggering statement. It goes against all of our natural instincts, and I know Jesus is not talking about abandonment or ignoring or dishonoring our family in any way. That would be totally against His teachings. But there are times when a choice has to be made to be away from family for a season for Kingdom purposes.

Of course, leaving family in this time zone is different than times past. At least, there is FaceTime. I have a grandson, Dominic, who lives in Guam. We FaceTime with him almost every week. One of the things I do to relieve the tension of us not being together physically is go into my comedy skit from "The Widow." And before you know it, we are both crackin' up thousands of miles away. He even tries to imitate me sometimes, which is hilarious at his young age. Even in this, *God is doing the impossible.*

Nothing ever takes the place of being with love ones, and I'm thankful to God that I can stay in touch and still carry on my work in the ministry for the Lord. If some could have predicted to the saints of old that God would inspire man to invent such a thing, they probably couldn't have wrapped their heads around that one. A much-needed technology and thank you, Lord, for this *hidden treasure* invention!

> "Everything that God told the prophets to write about the Son of Man will happen. He will be handed over to the foreigners, who will laugh at him, insult him, and spit on him. They will beat him with whips and then kill him. But on the third day after his death, he will rise to life again." The apostles tried to understand this, but they could not; the meaning was hidden from them. (Luke 18:31–34)

(LP) The Blink

So all that one goes through has an ending point and then we rise to a new life I call *the Blink.*

To the person who passes away, death is like a blink because there's no time at the moment you enter eternity, which doesn't have a clock attached to it. Can you remember the thousands of years before you came to this planet? It's like you've always been here right.

You don't even realize that you just started to exist thirty, forty, fifty, sixty years ago. Then we were coming out of our mother's womb, kicking and screaming. Scriptures say, "To be *absent from the body, is to be present with the Lord.*" Death is but a blink. And then we're in the presence of the Lord! The Rise is going to happen—and it will be glorious.

Putting it another way, this is the time of God's resurrection for you, my friend. Rise…Rise…Rise…it's your time. The time you have spent, searching, striving, stretching to attain your appointed position has been duly noted. And now it springs forth like a geyser in Yellowstone Park. I can hear the sound of it rushing up from below, anxious to reach the surface, promoted by a natural pressure that not even scientist can explain. Higher and higher you rise with much-needed moisture in your wings for a dry and thirsty world. Now the *treasure* has been *hidden* long enough. Open up the *hidden treasures* so the world can spend the wealth of your years and experiences. And for all you have been through, you'll look back and it will seem like only a *blink*!

> "Son of David, please help me!"
> Jesus stopped there and said, "Bring that man to me!" When he came close, Jesus asked him, "What do you want me to do for you?"
> He said, "Lord, I want to see again."
> Jesus said to him, "You can see now. You are healed because you believed."
> Then the man was able to see. He followed Jesus, thanking God. Everyone who saw this praised God for what happened. (Luke 18:39–43)

(LP) Time with You

One quality I want to instill in my followers, friends, and fans is that as soon as my name is mentioned, come rushing to wherever I am. The reason I am near you is to impart something special that the Lord wants to give you to help with your life. This has always been my private prayer, for God to make every moment we share together a right-now moment in time. The message in the music always takes time to develop and has a season of release after many days, weeks, and months of incubation.

I always pray that the Spirit be thick in that place where we gather together as if we have all put on 3D glasses that reveals a new and exciting dimension of God. And may we leave our *time* together, not only satisfied but may a light be turned on that wasn't there before of direction and confirmation. That our *time* together will be stone-sharping stone. A *hidden treasure* revealed each time we think of each other.

There are now studies on living in the now, which from days past was simply listening to people when they talk, giving eye contact when talking to someone as opposed to staring off in space like the person is not there or hearing what the other is saying, or even reading between the lines when they can't quite articulate their emotions. It is known by a few names: mindfulness, present moment, nowness, to name a few.

UCLA studies have put it this way: "Mindfulness is an excellent antidote to the stresses of modern life. It is the art of paying attention to present moment experiences with openness and curiosity. Mindfulness can be developed through meditation practice, and it is also a quality of attention that can be brought to any moment in life. It can be employed throughout the day to deal with stressful situations and to reduce emotional reactivity. Mindfulness tools and practices can help us with work, family, relationships, health, and in any areas of stress and difficulty. Anyone of any background can be taught mindfulness to find more ease and well-being, no matter what life's circumstances."

I thought this was a pretty modern way of saying don't let the bad memories of the past dictate your future and know that life is a journey on the way to your destination. Since, according to scripture, "everywhere our feet touch, is Holy Ground." We can also have "God's presence" in our every waking moments, which when this is applied, you are mindful (if you want to use that word) of all you can contribute to each moment and each person you encounter. That alone can shape a day and the day's activities with a new awareness and exuberance.

Now that everyone has a cell phone, you can pull up experiences that can bring a moment of calm, joy, and even humor. Even you're favorite Scriptures at the touch of your fingers. Saints of old would be laughing at us with all these tools and still having such deep issues in our lives. I say this because there were no heaters in the cool of the night, no air conditioners in the heat of the day, no microwave, in fact no oven or fridge. Everything had to be bought or shot daily. I'm not trying to paint a grim picture of our forefathers but just a reality check to say we've got more options to carry a bright Spirit into each day and be thankful and grateful for each moment we experience, with whomever or wherever we might be. In each moment you become a "treasure in someone else's field."

Luke 19

Jesus said, "Today is the day for this family to be saved from sin. Yes, even this tax collector is one of God's chosen people The Son of Man came to find lost people and save them."

—Luke 19:9–10)

(LP) Find Lost People

This is the point of it all—"To find lost people and save them." I was trained in my early days of following the Lord that I needed to go after anyone who would listen to His message. In the first year I was working with Glad Tidings Temple, the Assembly of God Church, where Richard was taking me. On the weekends, we would go down on Market Street in San Francisco and give them the gospel first, then we would give them a good meal. Now, forty-two years later, I'm associated with the Impact Center here in Vegas that is providing the same type of service.

It's amazing to me how much the Lord loves people. I get a glimpse of it, especially in this sort of environment. I pray that the body of Christ as a whole would continue to be sensitive for *lost people*. If we don't, we need to spend a little more time in prayer and ask our Heavenly Father just how we can be used in that capacity. Even though our outreach my not seem to be as big or far reaching as some. It is still necessary in the overall plan of our Lord. Every one of us on this planet are valuable to Him.

We recently stayed with an older couple that had three pictures on their fridge. They were kids from third world countries that they support every month. The kids are not saved but in need of so many things like food, shelter, and clothing. Things we take for granted.

There was a survey taken that says, if all of us Christian were to give 10 percent of our income, we could end world hunger, which is a startling statistic.

Some believe that there is no God. That's why our presence in the world is so vital. The Body of Christ could be the only physical human extension of His existence.

Joke: A couple had two little mischievous boys, ages eight and ten. They were always getting into trouble, and their parents knew that if any mischief occurred in their town, their sons would get the blame. The boys' mother heard that a clergyman in town had been successful in disciplining children, so she asked if he would speak with her boys. The clergyman agreed and asked to see them individually. So the mother sent her eight-year-old first in the morning, with the older boy to see the clergyman in the afternoon.

The clergyman, a huge man with a booming voice, sat the younger boy down and asked him sternly, "Where is God?" The boy's mouth dropped open, but he made no response, sitting there with his mouth hanging open. The clergyman repeated the question. "Where is God?" Again, the boy made no attempt to answer. So the clergyman raised his voice some more and shook his finger in the boy's face and bellowed, "Where is God!" The boy screamed and bolted from the room. He ran directly home and dove into his closet, slamming the door behind him. When his older brother found him in the closet, he asked, "What happened?" The younger brother, gasping for breath, replied, "We are in real *big* trouble this time! God is missing, and they think we did it!"

"God's not dead," saints. He's living in us. He is the *hidden treasure* that lost people are looking for!

> But the man was made king. When he came home, he said, "Call those servants who have my money. I want to know how much more money they earned with it." The first servant came and said, "Sir, I earned ten bags of money with the one bag you gave me." The king said to him, "That's great! You are a good servant. I see that I

can trust you with small things. So now I will let
you rule over ten of my cities." (Luke 19:15–17)

(LP) Use It or Lose It

This is the challenge of life—to take what Christ has given
us and multiply it. It was important enough for Him to put into
scripture. Does that mean every single thing? Good question. But
it definitely applies to business and many other important aspects
of our lives—our job skill or our athletic abilities, school studies,
and definitely our ministry endeavors. Anything where we can cause
advancement, we should! It's a *hidden treasure*.

Case in point below:

> The king said, "People who use what they have
> will get more. But those who do not use what
> they have will have everything taken away from
> them. Now where are my enemies? Where are the
> people who did not want me to be king? Bring
> my enemies here and kill them. I will watch them
> die." (Luke 19:26–27)

(LP) To Further Emphasis the Point!

> The two followers went into town. They found
> the donkey exactly like Jesus told them. They
> untied it, but its owners came out. They said
> to the followers, "Why are you untying our
> donkey?"
> The followers answered, "The Master needs
> it." So the followers brought the donkey to Jesus.
> They put their coats on its back. Then they put
> Jesus on the donkey. He rode along the road
> toward Jerusalem. The followers spread their
> coats on the road before him. (Luke 19:32–36)

(LP) So Fear Is Laughing, Keep Laughing Back

You see, even Jesus had to borrow things from others to use for his ministry. And He had such honor and integrity attached to His name that His need for the donkey was never even questioned. So this sets things straight for all time concerning asking people for things that will make all the difference for ministry.

When we have FEAR (Faith Eroding After Rejection), the rejection can even start before you make an actual phone call. Your mind tries to play out a scenario in which you fail. It even tries to convince you that you have already failed by even thinking of such an impossible thing.

So your faith starts to erode like a beautiful house on top of the mountain that so-called experts say will wash away with the next rainy season. But even scholars that we look up to can get it wrong. Faith does not play by those same rules. For one, our Foundation (All Mighty God) does not erode, and everything He has created grows into a more solid form, as His unlimited power and abilities accompany it.

I just heard a professional life coach say that a few millionaires were interviewed to find their common thread for success. All of them said, the same thing—that they had written down their specific goals for life and stayed the course, regardless of their competition or opposition.

My new song, "Ready to Rise" says,
"So fear is laughing, keep laughing back
Ha-ha-ha-ha-ha-ha, stay right on track.
This is your season, don't compromise
That gift inside of you is ready to rise.
Higher, Higher, Higher, Higher, Higher Higher,
Ready to Rise."

"Eye has not seen, nor ear heard, nor has it entered the heart of man, the things that God has prepared for those who love Him, and are called according to His purpose." A *hidden treasure* will refute a

FEAR-filled day. Even if you have fear, teachers and philosophers say, take fear on in with you, to your meeting or sales calls. I have had some of the most successful meetings where sweat would literally be rolling down from under my arms. I make a habit now of purposely wearing black shirts in those type of occasions.

> "Some of the Pharisees said to Jesus, 'Teacher, tell your followers not to say these things.' But Jesus answered, 'I tell you, if my followers didn't say them, these stones would shout them'" (Luke 19:39–40).

(LP) Oh, Happy Day

When Jesus has someone or something set to praise Him, nothing can stop that act. But if some self-centered rebellious organism refuses, someone else will step up and praise Him without even a millisecond loss. Maybe a scientist, in the very near future.

I have witnessed in my lifetime acts of God that were completely positioned by His plan. For instance, the song written by my friend Edwin Hawkins, "Oh Happy Day." Edwin says, "The song was recorded at the Ephesians Church of God in Christ, in my hometown of Oakland, California, to raise money for the church youth choir to attend a convention. We were going to hand sell the album in the Bay Area. We ordered five hundred copies. Lamont Bench, a Mormon guy, recorded that album on a two-track system. All five hundred copies sold." He continues, "One of those albums fell into the hands of Abe Voco Keshishian, an influential DJ at KSAN FM in the Bay Area, who started to play the song on his Lights Out San Francisco Blues and Rock program. Then, Dan Sorkin, a morning DJ at powerhouse station KSFO AM radio, was the proving ground for pop music in San Francisco, began pushing the song as well. The song created enough of a stir on the West Coast that sixteen record labels started bidding on rights to release the song nationally with Buddha Records winning the bid. I wasn't planning to go into the music business, and I wasn't looking for a record deal. *The record's success decided my fate!*"

The rest was history as the song caught fire on pop signals from coast to coast and even crossed over to R & B radio. What made "Oh Happy Day" resonated is anyone's guess, says the writer. But this song was designed and orchestrated by divine power. It's the only way to explain it.

As a footnote to the Christian community, Edwin said this: "'Oh Happy Day' was like nothing in mainstream gospel music at the time and was controversially jarring to many in black church circles. We preach and the Bible teaches to take the gospel into all the world, but when it all comes down, we don't want to do that with our music." Hawkins said at the time, "And the church world is quick to criticize that I think sometimes it is out of jealousy. Someone has succeeded, and people don't like it. A lot of that goes on."

Thank you, Edwin, for your song. It will continue to be evidence of how God can defy the laws of nature, because in actuality, He is the creator of those laws. Your legacy lives on, my friend. A *hidden treasure* that will continually live in my heart and stir up the gifts within me.

> Jesus came near Jerusalem. Looking at the city, he began to cry for it and said, "I wish you knew today what would bring you peace. But it is hidden from you now. A time is coming when your enemies will build a wall around you and hold you in on all sides. They will destroy you and all your people. Not one stone of your buildings will stay on top of another. All this will happen because you did not know the time when God came to save you." (Luke 19:41–44)

(LP) Our Gift Is a Power Source in God's Hands

Boy, that's a stark reality—the repercussion of rejecting JC. For me, it's another reason to step up my spirit and be as engaged in my art form as I can. Just the mere not doing of a call could be like a rejection of our Savior.

I was called upon to work with the Good News club here in Vegas. And they held a concert at the Cashman Center featuring yours truly. It had all the challenges and opportunities of a secular concert, but now that it was here, I wondered what I would do. I called my friends William and Jane at the Astudia Dance World Studios and told them about the opportunity. They immediately agreed to work with me on this new venture.

At the time, I was working on songs for the new genre of music album *Ready 2 Rise* and thought I would try a few out on the audience. It came off so good, I was encouraged by many to start a show here in Vegas that would be more family friendly. At the release of this book, the Leon Patillo Sanctuary is being formed now, for the strip. We would be the *hidden treasure* in this city and a place of safety for saints and others visiting from all over the world. *A power source in God's hands.*

> Jesus went into the Temple area. He began to throw out the people who were selling things there. He said, "The Scriptures say, 'My Temple will be a house of prayer.' But you have changed it into a hiding place for thieves."
>
> Jesus taught the people in the Temple area every day. The leading priests, the teachers of the law, and some of the leaders of the people wanted to kill him. But they did not know how they could do it, because everyone was listening to him. The people were very interested in what Jesus said. (Luke 19:45–48)

(LP) When You've Done All to Stand…Stand Therefore!

One of the messages our Lord is conveying here is consistency—that's the beauty of the church and its long history.

I speak to the pastors right now! I know you've spent a lot of years in ministry and your church hasn't seemed to be growing. Just keep remembering that in God's puzzle box, there are big pieces and little pieces. But when the puzzle is all put together, it makes a beautiful portrait. You are part of a bigger plan that involves you specifically. Have you ever seen a portrait with a few pieces missing? It doesn't have the same beauty or quality!

You know this to be true in your counseling sessions. Your words and counsel can make the difference between life and death. You are valued, my friend, by so many that may never be able to tell you how much they love and appreciate you. So let me say it, in the words of a song:

> "All of me, loves all of you, correcting my direction, loving me through my imperfection.
> You gave your all to me, I give my all to you.
> You're my end and my beginning, even when I lose I'm winnin'...
> I give you all, all, all of me...
> 'cause you gave me all, all, all of you!"
> (Leon Patillo Christian Version on YouTube)

Imagine all your congregation standing in unity and singing this song to you. These words are how we all feel about you, Pastor, and we are so proud of your faithfulness, all these many years. And one day your reward will be greater and more overwhelming than you could have ever imagined!

I also like how Jesus stepped up his game and didn't worry about popularity. And in the end, the scripture says, "*The people were very interested in what Jesus said.*" A bold stand always let's people know what you're all about, and they can choose to like you or not. The honest thing to do is be true to yourself and your branding because God has made all of us unique in some way.

You'll find in life that whatever muscle you develop over time are the ones that show up consistently. Honesty is not all that bad. Joan Rivers made a good living at it, and people liked her right up until she left out. It may not be the best example, but it is a great point. *When you've done all to stand...stand therefore!* Honesty and following our call is one of the most powerful *hidden treasures*.

Luke 20

One day Jesus was in the Temple area teaching the people. He was telling them the Good News. The leading priests, teachers of the law, and older Jewish leaders came to talk to Jesus. They said, "Tell us what authority you have to do these things. Who gave you this authority?" Jesus answered, "I will ask you a question too. Tell me: When John baptized people, did his authority come from God or was it only from other people?"

—Luke 20:1–4

(LP) Raw Gifts Are Needed Too

Interestingly, this line of questioning even happened when Jesus was twelve so he knew how to counteract their rebuttal. Jesus was not only the Son of God but a wise orator too.

I don't know if you picked up on this, but it was never stated if John went to seminary or not. His calling seemed to not need those credentials. And that's interesting in that he was the forerunner for Jesus and had the awesome privilege to baptize Him. So for some of you who think you have to be certified to be a powerful tool in God's hand, think again. *Raw gifts are needed too.* In fact, your *raw gift* may make the difference in how you convey the Gospel as opposed to the schooled. I have said this on more than one occasion that when I visit the prisons, the Christian men there have such a love and tenacity for Christ, that I wonder who's schooling who! Any one of them could get up and take over the meeting and give us a sermon full of meat. It could be because they have a day-to-day exercise in real-life application! A *raw* message from your heart or real-life experiences speaks volumes—and is a valuable *hidden treasure*.

> "So Jesus said to them, 'Then I will not tell you who gave me the authority to do these things'" (Luke 20:8).

(LP) Fruit Is Enough

So he never answered their question. There will be times in our lives when we don't have to explain ourselves either, especially if we are centered in God's will. That's enough right there to build authority on. What better stamp could you have than fruit? Instead of spending a lot of time flashing your credentials (of which I wholeheartedly believe in or I wouldn't have gone through it), flash your fruit! I don't mean flash 'em, but let their changed lives be your testimony. That, my friend, is true authority mixed with *hidden treasures*.

> The owner of the vineyard said, "What will I do now? I will send my son. I love my son very much. Maybe the farmers will respect my son." When the farmers saw the son, they said to each other, "This is the owner's son. This vineyard will be his. If we kill him, it will be ours." So the farmers threw the son out of the vineyard and killed him.
> What will the owner of the vineyard do? He will come and kill those farmers. Then he will lease the land to some other farmers. (Luke 20:13–16)

(LP) Everything Is on Loan

It's the story of the whole Bible: God sending his love in multiple ways and man being given more than he deserves. Those of us that respond back, bless Him so much.

Also, note that those working in the vineyard thought they would inherit the land. That must have been the dark one's thoughts too when he was thrust upon this planet! But the workers were not the original owners anyway. What were they thinking or drinking? *Everything is on loan.*

That also translates toward our mate and children who God has *loaned* to us. We don't own them, even our houses can take a turn in a bad economy! I have even heard of people that are renting who start thinking it's their house until they miss their rent payment a few times and that dreaded rent termination letter comes!

Lord, we honor you today concerning all our possessions. Anything we have is a product of your grace and mercy. No matter how talented or what skills of ingenuity we have, all things come from you. And in you, oh Lord, we live and move and have our being. Help us to be good stewards of what we have and always give you credit for it all. May we be found worthy, as we enter the final phase of life, leaving a legacy for many to continue to build on. And most of all, to hear you say, "Well done, good and faithful servant. Come and see what I've prepared for you." This will be when all our *hidden treasures* will be hidden no more!

> "But Jesus knew that these men were trying to trick him. He said to them, 'Show me a silver coin. Whose name and picture are on it?' They said, 'Caesar's.' He said to them, 'Then give to Caesar what belongs to Caesar, and give to God what belongs to God'" (Luke 20:23–25).

(LP) Both Realms Have a Part to Play in God's Overall Plan

I absolutely love this scripture, which is all inclusive. You don't have to defy the world system to accomplish God's work. You simply identify it as to what it is. There is a world existence and a spiritual kingdom existence. They both can coexist. Taxes make it possible for government to take care of our programs and national security needs, and God has got his design for mankind's soul and destiny!

In my music, I am building a "bridge" to get the two parts to cross to each other. Both are meant to accomplish the advancement of mankind. There shouldn't be a resistance. When someone says taxes, we just settle in and get the job done. If someone says give thanks and gratitude to God, settle in and get the job done. *Both realms have a part to play in God's overall plan.*

There are some things we build, based on math, architecture, and science. Some things we build that are being held together by something we don't see, like radio waves and air, of which even planes need in the right proportion to fly!

The amazing story of Charles Blondin, a famous French tight-rope walker, is a wonderful illustration of balance between the physical world and faith. Blondin's greatest fame came on September 14, 1860, when he became the first person to cross a tightrope stretched eleven thousand feet (over a quarter of a mile) across the mighty Niagara Falls. People from both Canada and America came from miles away to see this great feat.

He walked across 160 feet above the falls several times, each time with a different daring feat: once in a sack, on stilts, on a bicycle, in the dark, and blindfolded. One time he even carried a stove and cooked an omelet in the middle of the rope!

A large crowd gathered and the buzz of excitement ran along both sides of the riverbank. As Blondin carefully walked across, one dangerous step after another, pushing a wheelbarrow holding a sack of potatoes. Upon reaching the other side, the crowd's applause was louder than the roar of the falls! Blondin suddenly stopped and addressed his audience, "Do you believe I can carry a person across in this wheelbarrow?"

The crowd enthusiastically yelled, "Yes! You are the greatest tightrope walker in the world. We believe!"

"Okay," said Blondin, "Who wants to get into the wheelbarrow."

As far as the Blondin story goes, no one did at the time!

Both realms have a part to play in God's overall plan. A wonderful *hidden treasure*. But I won't be walking over a tightrope any time soon.

> Jesus said to the Sadducees, "On earth, people marry each other. Some people will be worthy to be raised from death and live again after this life. In that life they will not marry. In that life people are like angels and cannot die. They are children of God, because they have been raised from death. Moses clearly showed that people are raised from death. When Moses wrote about the burning bush, he said that the Lord is 'the God of Abraham, the God of Isaac, and the God of Jacob.' So they were not still dead, because he is the God only of living people. Yes, to God they are all still living."
>
> Some of the teachers of the law said, "Teacher, your answer was very good." (Luke 20:34–39)

(LP) So What's Next?

It's interesting that the marriage issue is only an earthly one. I'm sure our Lord will have another suitable arrangement concerning love in heaven. The one he came up with on this side of heaven was pretty cute, especially the way he kicked it off with Adam and Eve. They didn't have to worry about food, clothing, shelter, or credit cards. Wow!

In the next life the body will be made up of such an imperishable material that it will be able to endure the journey through time, a body that will never die again. Wow, to have an eternal life span— hard to wrap a human brain around that one.

I'm sure whatever your arrangements will be, Lord, will be just fine with me. I already know that you are preparing a mansion. But, of course, beyond all this, Jesus, You will be there! The most exciting *hidden treasure* of them all.

"In the book of Psalms, David himself says, 'The Lord God said to my Lord: Sit by me at my right side, and I will put your enemies under your power'" (Luke 20:42–43).

(LP) Get Ready to Conduct an Orchestra!

Yes, Lord. Yes, Lord. Yes, yes, Lord, Amen. Any enemy known or unknown, foreign or domestic, be put under your power, Lord. Because it is a power struggle, and you, our Father, which art in Heaven, You are the most powerful force in the universe.

God has given us the conductor's stick and with it is the ability to bring in certain instruments at the right time. Some don't play for a season, and then at the appropriate time, the whole orchestra is brought in. And with every player on the team playing to their best and highest ability, the atmosphere will change.

Wikipedia says it this way: "Conducting is the art of directing a musical performance, such as an orchestral or choral concert. The primary duties of the conductor are to interpret the score created by a composer in a manner which is reflective of those specific indications within that score, set the tempo, ensure correct entries by various members of the ensemble, and to "shape" the phrasing where appropriate. To convey their ideas and interpretation, a conductor communicates with their musicians primarily through hand gestures, typically though not invariably with the aid of a baton, and may use other gestures or signals, such as eye contact with relevant performers. A conductor's directions will almost invariably be supplemented or reinforced by verbal instructions or suggestions to their musicians in rehearsal prior to a performance."

This I'm sure is a prototype of how God conducts the universe. The Bible opens with the words, "In the beginning God created..." This dramatic statement declares God to be the eternal source and foundation of all that is. The Bible proceeds to reveal the person, nature, and character of the triune God who forever is Father, Son, and Holy Spirit.

Nature of God

We believe in one sovereign, true, and living God, creator and preserver of all things. God knows all things, is all-powerful, and transcends time and space. God is a personal being, revealing His righteousness, truth, and grace to all people. He calls everyone to respond to Him in reverence and obedience. God is perfect, just, and good. God is holy, calling us to righteousness. God is love, bridging the distance between Himself and us, reaching out in redemption to draw us to Himself.

God's self-disclosure has been progressive. Even though God transcends human perception and language, He has revealed Himself in Scripture, entered human history in the person of Jesus Christ, and comes to live in us by the Holy Spirit. As God opens our understanding by the Scriptures and by the Holy Spirit, we gain knowledge of Him. Thus, as believers, we bow before Him in worship.

Creation and Providence

God created all things, visible and invisible, including all spiritual beings. All creation is finite and dependent upon the Creator, who was before all things and will continue forever.

God's work of creation was good, both physically and morally. God blessed creation with His loving-kindness. Although God upholds and governs creation by the power of His will, God has given humanity the role of caretaker of the earth. Therefore, we are responsible for its cultivation and preservation and our use of its resources.

Creation was marred as a result of human disobedience. However, evidence of creation's original order remains, and the earth now awaits restoration in God's redemptive plan.

Relationships in Creation

God established order and relationships within His creation, uniting it in all its parts. God created and sustains all things, yet remains distinct from what is created. God does not depend on the creation for His being.

A moral order exists in the universe. The human conscience senses this order, which is more fully revealed in the Scriptures. The moral principles set forth in the Scriptures provide direction for our conduct and relationships.

The Creator has built a cycle of work and rest into the creation, one day in seven being designated by God for worship and renewal. By observing Sunday as the Lord's Day or Saturday for the Seventh Day Adventist, we honor this divinely-ordained cycle, testify of our trust in God's provision, and witness to the Lord's resurrection.

Made in God's image, each human being is of infinite value and is to be cared for and nurtured. We should relate to others in love and justice, opposing that which destroys, oppresses, demeans, or manipulates, and fostering that which restores, up builds, and affirms. God's plan for the human family calls for wholesome growing relationships among all persons. It forbids abusive and destructive behavior.

God gave human sexuality a good place in creation. Being either male or female is integral to who we are and in a complementary way provides for the full expression of our humanity. God has given standards for expression of our sexuality that are necessary for proper relationships among people. Human sexuality is affirmed within the chaste single life or a lifelong marriage between a man and a woman.

Personal Note: Even though this is the biblical view, I won't let this interfere with my love for the LGBTQ community. There is a lot to be accomplished concerning relationships between all people and our Savior—and love has to remain in the center of it all.

Supporting Scripture:

God and Creation: Genesis 1–2, Psalm 24:1–2, Hebrews 11
Nature of God: Deuteronomy 6:4, 32:3–4, 33:27; Psalm 45:6, 48:14, 100:5; Daniel 6:26–27; Matthew 3:16–17; John 14:16–17, 26; Acts 14:15–17; 1 Corinthians 2:11–16; Ephesians 2:8–10; 1 Timothy 1:17; James 1:17; Revelation 16:7

Creation and Providence: Genesis 1–3; 1 Chronicles 29:11–12; Nehemiah 9:6; Job 26:7–11; Psalm 19, 102:25; Romans 5:12–19; Hebrews 1:3; Revelation 19:6

Relationships in Creation: Genesis 1–2; Exodus 20:1–17; Leviticus 19:18; Deuteronomy 16:20; Psalm 104:24; Proverbs 21:3; Isaiah 58:13–14; Micah 6:8; Malachi 2:16; Matthew 12:8; 19:1–12, 25:40; Mark 2:27; Romans 2:13–15, 14:5–6; 1 Corinthians 6:9–10; Ephesians 4:29–5:2, 5:21–6:4; Colossians 1:16–17; 1 John 3:14, *Brethren in Christ*

Personal Note

During this life, may I continue to enlarge my ability to bring into the band every conceivable instrument, even beyond the music—TV, movies, sitcoms, Internet, books, concerts, young artist, speaking engagements, videos, and future endeavors yet to be revealed. My baton is ready and is at your disposal, oh Lord. And I know the reason I'm holding it is really on loan from you, my Savior. Let your wand compel the environment around me.

My power over the enemy is my ability to pursue with my conductor's stick in the face of unconceivable odds—above the orchestra and band leaders that have chosen to represent a negative viewpoint. I receive that power now and activate it *now*. My mouth and my spirit joined together to strike with a force greater than any know phenomenon known to mankind. The harvest is *huge*, but the laborers are few. Bring now the harvesters, Lord, for the greatest harvest of all time. To set in place a style that will be a foundation stone for all generations to stand on! Amen!

Unleash the *hidden treasure in my field*.

Luke 21

They have plenty, and they gave only what they did not need. This woman is very poor, but she gave all she had to live on.

—Luke 21:4)

(LP) A Little Can Count for a Lot

In those days they had a brass tube shaped like a very large trumpet. When they came into the synagogue, they would place the offering up high where the mouthpiece was situated. And as the coins, traveled down the brass tube, the whole place could hear the offering. That's why it was so amazing to these people to believe that such a small offering could represent more than those that woke up the whole congregation with their gift. It was such a humble feat that God made it a part of scripture. May this be the goal of all of us saints, Lord! That we will give you the best that we have and not just the leftovers.

As Christensen scrolled down the homepage of the Bike Rack, a shop in their town of St. Charles, Illinois, a video link for Project Mobility caught her eye. She clicked on it out of curiosity. The clip told how Bike Rack co-owner Hal Honeyman had created an organization to provide specially engineered bicycles to people with disabilities. It showed the happy faces of those who were now riding them: accident victims, injured veterans, and children with disabilities, including Hal's own son, who had been born with cerebral palsy.

"I'm going to buy a bike for one of those kids," Riley told her mother. Two days later she showed Christensen a letter she had written asking for donations. "I think it's amazing for a guy to make bikes for kids who can't walk," the letter said. "I saw how happy a boy was when he got one…I'm writing to ask for your help."

Christensen was blown away by her daughter's effort, but doubts quickly emerged. The cost of just one of those special bikes could be as high as $4,000. Riley could never raise the money. Nonetheless, her letter went out to seventy-five relatives and friends. Within three days, checks and cash began arriving. Then word got around about Riley's campaign, and as Christmas neared, more and more donations rolled in. The teen ultimately raised more than $12,000—enough to pay for seven bikes.

Last Christmas Eve, Riley delivered the bicycles to three of the lucky kids: Ava, a thirteen-year-old girl with spina bifida; Jenny, a fifteen-year-old girl with cerebral palsy; and Rose, a four-year-old girl with a rare genetic disorder. "This is the best Christmas I ever had," said Riley.

She and Ava have since ridden together. "When I ride, I like to go fast, get sweaty, and feel the breeze," Riley says. "So does Ava. She pumps with her arms, not her feet, but she really flies."

Riley is determined to keep her campaign going every holiday season. "I want kids to feel the wind in their faces," she says.

A little can count for a lot—the perfect gift and *hidden treasure*.

> Some followers asked Jesus, "Teacher, when will these things happen? What will show us that it is time for these things to happen?"
>
> Jesus said, "Be careful! Don't be fooled. Many people will come using my name."
>
> Then Jesus said to them, "Nations will fight against other nations. Kingdoms will fight against other kingdoms. There will be great earthquakes, sicknesses, and other bad things in many places. In some places there will be no food for the people to eat. Terrible things will happen, and amazing things will come from heaven to warn people." (Luke 21:7–11)

(LP) Tough Love

As you can tell, we are having a lot of strange phenomenon in our world today. There are places that are having earthquakes that have never had them in reported history. In some third world countries, there are diseases that are killing whole villages at a time. Even those traveling to the regions and have had contact with the infected have to go into quarantine for a season when they come home. And some disease have no cure at all!

The time is slowly approaching as a nation where the rules of decency are changing and the moral standards are being replaced by feelings instead of facts. I never thought I would live long enough to see our court system ignore the ideals of our Founding Fathers and would bend to intimidation and whining.

I get all these outward signs and warnings. But this pathway to death and destruction is a spiritual thing. Our hope for the future will depend on if we can wake up in time and see the era of our ways. As stated earlier, we are renters at most on this planet. There is more at stake than the eye can conceive.

Lord, I intercede for our world right now and the people in it. As the field worker asked the landowner, "Give the tree more time to bear fruit," may we wake up just in time to escape a Noah-type episode. Help the heart of mankind to be moved by your mercy and grace where a true show of solidarity and commitment can become a reality. Sometimes these prayers are hard to pray, especially in light of the impending scriptures above. But I know you, Lord, I've seen your heart change, like it did for Jonah. He did suffer for a few days, but after his ordeal with the fish, he was spit out to continue his mission.

At the least, Lord, let us have real receptivity from our youth. May they get it and implement it instantaneously! They are our best hope for the future. They are the *hidden treasure* waiting to spill the whole treasury on to the world for our survival.

"Let the words of my mouth and the meditation of my heart be acceptable in thy sight, oh Lord." One whisper from you and the earth shakes in awe. "You are my strength and my redeemer."

Decide now not to worry about what you will say. I will give you the wisdom to say things that none of your enemies can answer. Even your parents, brothers, relatives, and friends will turn against you. They will have some of you killed. Everyone will hate you because you follow me. But none of these things can really harm you. You will save yourselves by continuing strong in your faith through all these things. (Luke 21:14–19)

(LP) Continue Strong in the Faith

I love that first line: "Decide now not to worry about what you will say." That's pretty cool to have that much confidence in your walk. But the key of it all is verse 19, *"You will save yourselves by continuing strong in your faith through all these things."* Why, because faith has a tendency to erode after rejection. *Fear* tries to convince you that there is no answer out there. But the Lord is reminding us to *continue strong in your faith through all these things.* And if someone, even someone in your circle, doubts what God has put on your heart, even more so, let it come to pass. It's up to our mouth and our heart to oppose it in the strictest terms. Why? Because in the final analysis, *no one knows* except Jesus. And since He has stayed the course till now, don't give up on the many years in the making for such a time as this. Amen.

Tyler Perry had a rough childhood. He was physically and sexually abused growing up, got kicked out of high school, and tried to commit suicide twice—once as a preteen and again at twenty-two. At twenty-three he moved to Atlanta and took up odd jobs as he started working on his stage career.

In 1992 he wrote, produced, and starred in his first theater production, *I Know I've Been Changed,* somewhat informed by his difficult upbringing. Perry put *all his savings* into the show, and it failed miserably. The run lasted just one weekend and only thirty people came to watch. He kept up with the production, working more odd jobs, and often slept in his car to get by. Six years later, Perry finally broke through when, on its seventh run, the show became a success. He's since gone on to have an extremely successful career as a director, writer, and actor. In fact, Perry was named *Forbes* highest paid man in entertainment in 2011.

Shania Twain's career actually began more out of necessity than raw ambition. Her parents divorced when she was two, and she rarely saw her father. Her mom and stepfather, to whom she grew close, often couldn't make enough to get by, so Twain started singing in bars to make extra money when she was just eight years old. She recalls her mother waking her up at all hours to get up and perform. Sadly, when she was twenty-one, her mother and stepfather were killed in a head-on car accident with a logging truck on the highway. Twain put her career on hold to step in and take care of her three younger siblings (who were in their teens at the time). She sang in resorts and put off going after big-time stardom until her sister and brothers were old enough to care for themselves. Only once her youngest brother graduated high school did she feel okay heading down to Nashville to pursue her career.

Oprah dealt with a lot throughout her public life: criticism about her weight, racism, intrusive questions about her sexuality, just to name a few. But she never let it get in the way of her ambition and drive. When you look at her childhood, her personal triumphs are cast in an even more remarkable light. Growing up, Oprah was reportedly a victim of sexual abuse and was repeatedly molested by her cousin, an uncle, and a family friend. Later, she became pregnant and gave birth to a child at age fourteen, who passed away just two weeks later. But Oprah persevered, going on to finish high school as an honor student, earning a full scholarship to college, and working her way up through the ranks of television, from a local network anchor in Nashville to an international superstar and creator of her OWN network.

Continue strong in the faith, my friend.
Amazing things will happen to the sun, moon, and stars. And people all over the earth will be upset and confused by the noise of the sea

and it's crashing waves. They will be afraid and
worried about what will happen to the world.
Everything in the sky will be changed. Then people will see the Son of Man coming in a cloud
with power and great glory. When these things
begin to happen, stand up tall and don't be afraid.
Know that it is almost time for God to free you!
(Luke 21:25–28)

(LP) Every Day Is One Step Closer to the Final Event

We as believers should always be excited because we are *one step
closer to the final event.* A time when hate will turn into love. Chaos
will turn into peace. Weapons of war will just be objects for the
museum. Angels will flutter and fill the atmosphere with the smell
of incense, which is the prayers of the saints, as all the nations and
tongues witness the appearance of the patriarchs of old.

And a voice so clear will pierce the air with a sound like a pleasant musical instrument and a calm will fill the atmosphere unlike
anything we've experienced before. And we shall see His face, the
one who was pierced for our transgressions, as He washes all the
tears from our eyes and lets us know that from this day forward, we
will always walk in His light with no more pain, no more sorrow, no
more fears and doubts. No more bills, hallelujah! And it will take all
eternity for Him to uncover all the *hidden treasures in his field* that
have been prepared since the foundation of the world.

> "I assure you that all these things will happen while
> some of the people of this time are still living. The
> whole world, earth and sky, will be destroyed, but
> my words will last forever" (Luke 21:32–33).

(LP) The Word: More Stable than Concrete

So again, we get the message of what is really stable on the
planet—God's word. That's why the dark side tries to underplay it

and get rid of it wherever possible, like schools and nativity scenes. Some are even proposing that only certain subject matters be discussed in the pulpit.

No matter how people put a spin on the validity of God's word, it will be the one to stand the test of time. Everything around us has and will fluctuate but not God's word. Drink it, eat it, quote it, stand on it, project it into your day, and make it the foundation for the future. As the script from the movie *Ten Commandments* says, "So let it be written, so let it be done."

Personal Note:

I just researched and found out that the *Ten Commandments* was the first movie I ever saw in a theater in 1956 when I was just nine years old. It began shaping my life then, and continues, even until today. That's another reason children need to be exposed to teaching from the Bible. It sets a tone for what the most powerful being in the universe has in store for their life. Which begs the question, why wouldn't the school system want the kids to have exposure to this valuable information and part of life? They want the best for the children, right? Even more importantly, a life with Christ is a life with endless possibilities.

God's Word is like a seed. We know because of what Jesus said.

Luke 8:11 (NKJ), "Now the parable is this: The seed is the word of God."

The Holy Spirit, through Peter, also said God's Word is a seed.

First Peter 1:23 (NKJ), "Having been born again, not of corruptible seed but incorruptible, through the word of God which lives and abides forever."

God's Word is alive, just like a seed. I even wrote a song about it, called "Thy Word" from the Worship and Healing Album.

John 6:63 (NKJ), "It is the Spirit who gives life; the flesh profits nothing. The words that I speak to you are spirit, and they are life."

Jesus said His words are alive. They contain life. The words in your Bible may look lifeless and powerless. Seeds do too. *The Word— more stable than concrete!*

In Mark 4:30–31 Jesus explained that the kingdom of God works like a seed. So if we are to understand God's kingdom and how He operates, we need to understand seeds.

Seeds:

A seed is alive: it contains life. Your physical senses are incapable of judging whether a seed is alive or not. You cannot see, feel, hear, smell, or taste the life in a seed. There is only one way to prove a seed is alive—plant it.

A seed does nothing until planted. Seeds do not grow sitting in a sack on your shelf. They must be planted in the proper place. If you desire the Word of God to produce in your life, *you* must decide to plant the Word in your heart and mind.

The best way to plant the seed of God's Word in your life is by speaking the Word. Hearing others speak the Word is good, but if you want a bountiful harvest, start speaking the Word yourself.

Romans 10:10 (NKJ), "For with the heart one believes to righteousness, and with the mouth confession is made to salvation."

A seed is much smaller than the plant it produces. The problem you face may seem huge. In comparison, a scripture may seem very small. But when planted, that Word will grow in you and overcome the problem.

A seed always produces what you plant.

Galatians 6:7 (NKJ), "Do not be deceived, God is not mocked; for whatever a man sows, that he will also reap."

Whatever you need, or desire, find scriptures relating to that. Then plant those scriptures inside of you in abundance. Those seeds will grow up and produce a harvest of what you need and sometimes desire.

A little seed is stronger than the forces around it. As a seed begins to grow, it will push up dirt and rocks, out of its way. Whatever the obstacles are, God's Word planted in your heart will push them out of the way.

A seed takes time to produce. No one expects a seed to produce a harvest the same day it's planted.

Sometimes the Word of God seems to spring up and bear fruit immediately. Yet if we knew the details of a person's life, we would hear that the fruit of the Word grew in that person's life over time.

A seed is persistent. A seed never gives up but works day and night. Even when you are sleeping, the seed you have planted is working to grow and express itself in a fruitful harvest.

A seed is not affected by other seeds. Whatever happens to other seeds does not make any difference to a specific seed. Each seed sticks to its own task. One wheat seed planted in a cornfield will still produce wheat. Seed does not become discouraged or quit even if other seeds die.

A seed will stop growing without nourishment. Planting a seed is not enough to assure a harvest. Seed must be protected and taken care of until harvest time. A seed which is dug up or not watered will not produce.

The more seeds planted, produce a larger harvest.

Second Corinthians 9:6 (NKJ), "But this I say: He who sows sparingly will also reap sparingly, and he who sows bountifully will also reap bountifully."

These little seeds (the Word) is more stable than concrete. Think on these truths about seeds. Allow the Holy Spirit to help you apply them to the role of God's Word in your life.

"During the day Jesus taught the people in the Temple area. At night he went out of the city and stayed all night on the Mount of Olives. Every morning all the people got up early to go listen to Jesus at the Temple" (Luke 21:37–38).

(LP) Listening to Gods Word Has Advantages

I had a season not long ago where I conducted a Bible study every morning during the week. It was only supposed to go for a month or so, but it ended up, lasting a year. It was quite a commitment for myself and those on the line. But even now I hear praise reports of how that time helped to realign the lives of the participants.

I heard a story once that goes something like this:

A young man went off to college and was having struggles with his daily needs. So he wrote his parents and explained his dilemma. They wrote him back and said, "Everything you need is in His Word, son." But he was insistent that he had been reading the Word, but his needs had not been met. This went on for months until finally the son decided to read the Scriptures to appease his parents. Well, to his surprise, when he opened the Bible to one of his favorite passages, a hundred dollars fell out. What had happened was his parents had put a hundred dollars in each chapter of each book of the Bible.

Of course, if we read the Bible, hundred dollar bills won't come flying out, but so much more. The value of God's word is inexhaustible and contributes history, promises, and future predictions. There is nothing like it, and His word will always be right on time for all our needs. I don't know anything else I could put my trust in with such certainty and full of *hidden treasures*.

> Jesus said to Peter and John, "Go and prepare the Passover meal for us to eat."
>
> They said to him, "Where do you want us to prepare the meal?"
>
> He said to them, "When you go into the city, you will see a man carrying a jar of water. Follow him. He will go into a house. Tell the owner of the house, 'The Teacher asks that you please show us the room where he and his followers can eat the Passover meal.' Then the owner will show you a large room upstairs that is ready for us. Prepare the meal there."

So Peter and John left. Everything happened the way Jesus said. So they prepared the Passover meal. (Luke 21:8–13)

(LP) Thank God, He Passed Over Us!

This was a big responsibility for these two to get right. In our Lord's mind's eye, He had the picture of the last supper picture already ingrained in his mind. It sounds like He wanted everything just right for Him and His disciples to spend their last meal together.

Like the disciples, I too feel a responsibility to give you what I have researched. It is an overview of Passover. It is a piece that I think will give you insight into this most holy event and that you may have to refer to from time to time. Sometimes these type of *hidden treasures* have to be unveiled to give us clarity, especially being such a historic event. So here we go:

Smith's Bible Dictionary: Passover

Passover, the first of the three great annual festivals of the Israelites, is celebrated in the month Nisan (March–April, from the fourteenth to the twenty-first (strictly speaking, the Passover only applied to the paschal supper and the feast of unleavened bread followed, which was celebrated to the twenty-first.). The following are the principal passages in the Pentateuch relating to the Passover: Exodus 12:1–51, 13:3–10, 23:14–19, 34:18–26; Leviticus 23:4–14; Numbers 9:1–14, 28:16–25, 16:1–6. Why is it instituted? This feast was instituted by God to commemorate the deliverance of the Israelites from Egyptian bondage and the sparing of their firstborn when the destroying angel smote the first-born of the Egyptians. The deliverance from Egypt was regarded as the starting point of the Hebrew nation. The Israelites were then raised from the condition of bondmen under a foreign tyrant to that of a free people owing allegiance to no one but Jehovah.

The prophet in a later age spoke of the event as a creation and a redemption of the nation. God declares himself to be "the Creator of

Israel." The Exodus was thus looked upon as the birth of the nation. The Passover was its annual birthday feast. It was the yearly memorial of the dedication of the people to him who had saved their firstborn from the destroyer in order that they might be made holy to himself.

First celebration of the Passover: On the tenth day of the month, the head of each family was to select from the flock either a lamb or a kid, a male of the first year, without blemish. If his family was too small to eat the whole of the lamb, he was permitted to invite his nearest neighbor to join the party. On the fourteenth day of the month, he was to kill his lamb while the sun was setting. He was then to take blood in a basin and with a sprig of hyssop to sprinkle it on the two side posts and the lintel of the door of the house. The lamb was then thoroughly roasted, whole. It was expressly forbidden that it should be boiled, or that a bone of it should be broken.

Unleavened bread and bitter herbs were to be eaten with the flesh. No male who was uncircumcised was to join the company. Each one was to have his loins girt to hold a staff in his hand and to have shoes on his feet. He was to eat in haste, and it would seem that he was to stand during the meal. The number of the party was to be calculated as nearly as possible so that all the flesh of the lamb might be eaten, but if any portion of it happened to remain, it was to be burned in the morning. No morsel of it was to be carried out of the house.

The lambs were selected on the fourteenth they were slain and the blood sprinkled, and in the following evening, after the fifteenth day, the first paschal meal was eaten. At midnight the firstborn of the Egyptians were smitten. The king and his people were now urgent that the Israelites should start immediately and readily bestowed on them supplies for the journey. In such haste did the Israelites depart on that very day (Num. 33:3) that they packed up their kneading troughs containing the dough prepared for the morrow's provisions, which was not yet leavened.

Observance of the Passover in later times: The head of the family slew the lamb in his own house, not in the holy place; the blood was sprinkled on the doorway, not on the altar. But when the law was perfected, certain particulars were altered in order to assimilate the

Passover to the accustomed order of religious service. In the twelfth and thirteenth chapters of Exodus, there are not only distinct references to the observance of the festival in future ages (e.g. Exodus 12:2, Exodus 12:14, Exodus 12:17, Exodus 12:24–27, Exodus 12:42, Exodus 13:2, Exodus 13:5, Exodus 13:8–10)

All work except that belonging to a few trades connected with daily life was suspended for some hours before the evening of the fourteenth Nisan. It was not lawful to eat any ordinary food after midday. No male was admitted to the table unless he was circumcised, even if he were of the seed of Israel (Exod. 12:48). It was customary for the number of a party to be not less than ten.

When the meal was prepared, the family was placed round the table. When the party was arranged the first cup of wine was filled, and a blessing was asked by the head of the family on the feast, as well as a special, one on the cup. The bitter herbs were then placed on the table and a portion of them eaten, either with or without the sauce. The unleavened bread was handed round next and afterward the lamb was placed on the table in front of the head of the family. The paschal lamb could be legally slain and the blood and fat offered only in the national sanctuary.(16:2). Before the lamb was eaten the second cup of wine was filled, and the son, in accordance with (Exod. 12:26) asked his father the meaning of the feast. In reply, an account was given of the sufferings of the Israelites in Egypt and of their deliverance, with a particular explanation of (26:5) and the first part of the Hallel (a contraction from Hallelujah). Psalm 113 and 114 was sung.

This being gone through, the lamb was carved and eaten. The third cup of wine was poured out and drunk, and soon afterward the fourth. The second part of the Hallel, Psalm 115 to 118 was then sung. A fifth wine-cup appears to have been occasionally produced, but perhaps only in later times. What was termed the greater Hallel, Psalm 120 to 138 was sung on such occasions. The Israelites who lived in the country appear to have been accommodated at the feast by the inhabitants of Jerusalem in their houses, so far if there was room for them.

(Matt. 26:18, Luke 22:10–12) Those who could not be received into the city encamped without the walls in tents as the pilgrims now do at Mecca. The Passover as a type. The Passover was not only commemorative but also typical. "The deliverance which it commemorated was a type of the great salvation it foretold." No other shadow of things to come contained in the law can vie with the festival of the Passover in expressiveness and completeness.

The paschal lamb must of course be regarded as the leading feature in the ceremonial of the festival. The lamb slain typified Christ, the Lamb of God, slain for the sins of the world. Christ "our Passover is sacrificed for us." (1 Cor. 5:7)

According to the divine purpose, the true Lamb of God was slain at nearly the same time as "the Lord's Passover" at the same season of the year; and at the same time of the day as the daily sacrifice at the temple, the crucifixion beginning at the hour of the morning sacrifice and ending at the hour of the evening sacrifice. That the lamb was to be roasted and not boiled has been supposed to commemorate the haste of the departure of the Israelites. It is not difficult to determine the reason of the command "not a bone of him shall be broken." The lamb was to be a symbol of unity—the unity of the family, the unity of the nation, the unity of God with his people whom he had taken into covenant with himself.

The unleavened bread ranks next in importance to the paschal lamb. We are warranted in concluding that unleavened bread had a peculiar sacrificial character, according to the law. It seems more reasonable to accept St, Paul's reference to the subject (1 Cor. 5:6–8) as furnishing the true meaning of the symbol. Fermentation is decomposition, a dissolution of unity. The pure dry biscuit would be an apt emblem of unchanged duration, and, in its freedom from foreign mixture, of purity also. The offering of the omer, or first sheaf of the harvest (Lev. 23:10–14) signified deliverance from winter the bondage of Egypt being well considered as a winter in the history of the nation. The consecration of the first-fruits, the firstborn of the soil, is an easy type of the consecration of the firstborn of the Israelites and of our own best selves to God.

Further than this the Passover is a type of deliverance from the slavery of sin. It is the passing over of the doom we deserve for your sins, because the blood of Christ has been applied to us by faith. The sprinkling of the blood upon the door posts was a symbol of open confession of our allegiance and love. The Passover was useless unless eaten, so we live upon the Lord Jesus Christ. It was eaten with bitter herbs, as we must eat our Passover with the bitter herbs of repentance and confession, which yet, like the bitter herbs of the Passover, are a fitting and natural accompaniment. As the Israelites ate the Passover all prepared for the journey, so do we with a readiness and desire to enter the active service of Christ and to go on the journey toward heaven!

Luke 22

*Then he took some bread and thanked God for it.
He broke off some pieces, gave them to the apostles
and said, "This bread is my body that I am giving
for you. Eat this to remember me." In the same way,
after supper, Jesus took the cup of wine and said,
"This wine represents the new agreement from God
to his people. It will begin when my blood is poured
out for you.*

—Luke 22:19–20

(LP) Remember Me

*This is a centerpiece statement of what Jesus wants us to do all day
long. Remember me!*

(LP) Serving Leads

This caption, may sound silly to a CEO of a company or a person, who has prided himself in being tops in his field. But the point is, *by serving, you lead better.*

People always emulate the person at the top. That's where most get their motivation and possibilities from. To put one's self lower than someone is the highest thing one can do! It literally changes both the person being served and the one doing the serving. J. C., the great teacher of all, was the one who set this pattern into motion.

In concert I generally take time to minister to couples. I make the biblical suggestion to men to serve their wives. I tell them that when the wife comes home from work or her domestic job to sit her down and ask her about her day. Turn off the TV, computer and cell phone, and really listen. Maybe prepare her a snack and a drink. After she has poured her heart out, come behind her, and massage her neck and shoulders. After that, go get some baby lotion, take off her shoes, and begin to massage her feet, in between those toes…oh yeah! Over and around those bunions…oh yeah!

When you think about it, us men are getting away with a better scenario than Jesus. He washed His disciples' feet, which I know was some nasty feet! A foot like that, no tellin' what little critter, might come runnin' out from in between those toes.

I was staying with Pastor John, who I want to call Rabbi John, which the only distinction is because he doesn't speak Hebrew. He is the pastor of a Messianic Jewish congregation in Idaho. After breakfast, this very wise and learned man, humbled himself and performed a foot washing ceremony on me. I was shocked because I have never had this happen to me before. I get man to woman, woman to man, but I've never had a brother from another mother do that to me!

It was a life-altering experience, and my overall demeanor took on a paradigm shift, and I could see others through new eyes! How refreshing and a new *hidden treasure*!

> "You men have stayed with me through many struggles. So I give you authority to rule with me in the kingdom the Father has given me. You will eat and drink at my table in that kingdom. You will sit on thrones and judge the twelve tribes of Israel" (Luke 22:28–30).

(LP) It Just Keeps Getting Better

Another reward, as if just having eternal life is not enough. He gives positions of authority to be like our Lord and co-labor with Him, even later. Wow! To co-labor with the supreme company with the most potential for growth is a no brainer. If mankind could catch a glimpse of this, it would be like the actor in the movie *Limitless* who took a special pill and became more aware and insightful about everything.

> "Satan has asked to test you men like a farmer
> tests his wheat. O Simon, Simon, I have prayed
> that you will not lose your faith! Help your
> brothers be stronger when you come back to me"
> (Luke 22:31–32).

(LP) Amazing Grace

When the whole world is shouting, "Crucify! Crucify!" God is yelling just as loud, "Father, forgive them, for they know not what they do." The mercy of our Lord is constantly on display and is the most outstanding expression of love I've ever encountered. It's like standing on the shore of the ocean as the sun is beating down on you, then suddenly a wave comes crashing over you to cool you off. As we take some stubborn stands in this life, I feel His mercy and grace crashing over me, a lot. Even though Jesus prayed for Simon, he still rebelled for a season. But in the end he became one of the most powerful of all the disciples.

The word GRACE has new meaning in light of this thinking: Giant Rebellion All Cancelled, Erased. A *hidden treasure* each time we slip!

> "But Peter said to Jesus, 'Lord, I am ready to go
> to jail with you. I will even die with you!' But
> Jesus said, 'Peter, before the rooster crows tomor-
> row morning, you will say you don't know me.
> You will say this three times'" (Luke 22:33–34).

(LP) Give Us More Consistency, Lord

We all make these kind of promises. Then we find ourselves in an environment sometimes where we feel a little shy about confessing his name. There is no doubt that we really love the Lord and are proud of all He has done in our lives. But God knows that we will fall short of that promise from time to time. I think that was what Jesus was trying to convey to Peter, that He knew the inconsistencies in his life and when it would happen. I think Peter was trying to say back that he would never go there. And I commend him for that type of passion.

It's such a blessing to know that even with all our inadequacies God's commitment to us will never change. In fact, His unchanging steadfast love shines brighter to us in those moments. A permanent *hidden treasure* tucked away in the heart of our Lord.

There have been some ordinary people that have done extraordinary feats of *consistency*. I think these stories will help you in that area and help you to push against all odds:

Brian Kolfage had been stationed at the Balad Air Base in Iraq for two weeks when an enemy rocket exploded three feet from where he was standing. His body felt like it was "lit on fire." His legs were destroyed, his right arm severed, and his survival was touch and go. But twelve months and sixteen surgeries later, the triple amputee was out of the hospital, reportedly as the most severely wounded airman to survive any war. Three years later, with three prosthetic limbs and new skills in his nondominant left hand, he enrolled in the competitive program at the University of Arizona's College of Architecture, where fewer than one in five applicants was accepted. On track to graduate in 2014, the Pat Tillman Scholarship recipient has a 3.8 GPA and hopes to "revolutionize military architecture." He noted, "I lost my legs, but I have my head, my brain. I can do everything I did before mentally."

Martha Mason graduated valedictorian of her high school and earned two college degrees at the top of the class—all while living her life in an iron lung. Paralyzed by polio at age eleven in 1948 and confined twenty-three hours a day in an immobile eight hundred--pound horizontal tube, the voracious reader stayed "endlessly curious" and amazingly adaptable. Custom-built intercoms connected her to school and made her a "regular member" in her classes, with the technology helping her from high school through Wake Forest College (now University), where the English major arrived at her dorm room in a bakery truck. By the time she died in 2009, Mason had been in the iron lung for a record-setting sixty years. "Something happens to all of us," she said in a documentary about her, *Martha in Lattimore.* "Mine is more visible than yours, but you have to deal with your things too. None of us are exempt from things that would make us extraordinary people if the world knew the story."

When faced with these incredible stories. We can't help but be more steadfast for our Lord, especially in light of not having these afflictions to deal with. It wasn't noted in the articles, but I'm sure their faith had a lot to do with keeping them on track with their goals. Look at how *consistent* our Lord has been with His vision for our lives. He knew when He made us that it was going to cost Him something. He wasn't surprised by Adam and Eve's sin and rebellion. He had a vision that involves you and I even now, in this present moment. If we can continue to walk with Him and talk with Him against all that we may have going on personally, I believe our Lord will get sweeter and sweeter with each day.

> Then Jesus said to the apostles, "Remember when I sent you out without money, a bag, or sandals? Did you need anything?"
>
> The apostles said, "No."
>
> Jesus said to them, "But now if you have money or a bag, carry that with you. If you don't have a sword, sell your coat and buy one." (Luke 22:35–36)

(LP) Be Prepared When God Moves a New Way

Maybe I didn't notice it before, but Jesus had weapons with Him (so Jesus was for bearing arms, hmmm.). But like everything else, you have to use them with discretion. Like when Peter cut off the soldier's ear, Jesus admonished him and told him that it was the wrong place and wrong time for that sort of use, or as we would say these days, excessive force. But it still blows me away that Jesus had a weapon. I just have never thought about it like that before, like a second amendment right.

And speaking of money bags, considering how our economy fluctuates, especially as an artist, I've been instructed to reinvent myself. In other words, *I'm preparing as God moves a new way!* It's a stretch, but when I think of how God reinvented himself from being the Creator of the world to becoming the lamb that was slain, I thank Him every day for making the alteration to die in our place.

I know as an artist, sometimes we can get stuck on our last hit that was three or four decades ago. Like my wife keeps telling me, if you have a new song to share, you better share it before all your fans transition to heaven.

Just thinking about Jesus the Creator becoming the lamb motivates me to offer myself as a sacrifice to the next generation. Then they can take the message, peer to peer, to their generation in the language they can understand.

I have been in *preparation* for this *new move* for quite some time. When the Lord is with me, I can make any change with His help. The credit should go to Him; the fruit will go to Him. And I believe our number one response to a *new move* is to be available. I don't know what your reinvention will be. But I can tell you with my call to children and to better health in the Body of Christ. It's a specific one, and I send out a text right now to my contemporaries—it's truly God's *hidden treasure*.

> Jesus left the city and went to the Mount of Olives. His followers went with him. (He went there often.) He said to his followers, "Pray for strength against temptation."
>
> Then Jesus went about steps away from them. He knelt down and prayed, "Father, if you are willing, please don't make me drink from this cup. But do what you want, not what I want." Then an angel from heaven came to help him. Jesus was full of pain; he struggled hard in prayer. Sweat dripped from his face like drops of blood falling to the ground. When he finished praying, he went to his followers. He found them asleep, worn out from their grieving. Jesus said to them, "Why are you sleeping? Get up and pray for strength…" (Luke 22:39–46)

(LP) Fifty Steps

What a great passage of scripture. *Fifty steps*, what a great reminder when we fall into temptation: walk fifty steps and pray. Not what I want, but what you want, Lord. Pray for strength against temptation. We don't realize the invisible forces that are all around us. Even in our minds, in our eye gate, in our unresolved heart issues. Oh, that we could take fifty steps and then deal with all the above in our lives. "Draw me nearer...near oh blessed Lord, to the place where thou hath died. Draw me nearer, near, oh blessed Lord to thou precious bleeding side." "Consecrate me now, in thy steadfast love." Fifty steps will be my forever *hidden treasure*.

Jesus said, "Stop!" Then he touched the servant's ear and healed him.

> Jesus spoke to the group that came to arrest him. They were the leading priests, the older Jewish leaders, and the Jewish soldiers. He said to them, "Why did you come out here with swords and clubs? Do you think I am a criminal? I was with you every day in the Temple area. Why didn't you try to arrest me there? But this is your time—the time when darkness rules." (Luke 22:51–53)

(LP) Light It Up! Darkness No Longer Rules

Even in Jesus's brief time on this earth, there was a darkness-rules episode. But Jesus was not only prepared but was the author of the outcome. All the scriptures past were pointing toward this show-down. And thank God, what Jesus did for us is irreversible. Light wins again.

Even this morning, the morning of a video shoot, the sun is just rising out of the east and darkness must give way to the light. Even the porch light from the house across the street that stands watch through the night gave way to the brighter light along with the other houses in this city in this northern hemisphere!

Darkness can come, but when light is there, it can't dominate. When the two forces meet and they are equal in proportion, there is no contest! Only if the light gives way to darkness, like Jesus did to make His ultimate sacrifice. I can imagine the look on the enemy's face when the surprise attack happened in Hades. When Jesus showed up and got the keys of hell, death, and the grave and lead captivity captive, exhibiting to us this reality—*Light it up; darkness no longer rules*—then bursting forth onto the face of the planet, alive and well from His ordeal, to regain his seat at the right hand of the Father, in full authority, as only the Son of God could do. Blessed be the name of the Lord!

> But Peter said, "Man, I don't know what you are talking about!"
>
> Immediately, while he was still speaking, a rooster crowed. Then the Lord turned and looked into Peter's eyes. And Peter remembered what the Lord had said, "Before the rooster crows in the morning, you will say three times that you don't know me." Then Peter went outside and cried bitterly. (Luke 22:60–62)

(LP) Thank God, He Knows Our True Heart

Whenever we deny our Lord in any way or in any setting, we are cut to the core of our being. It's the last thing any one of us believers wants to do, especially in light of what He has done and continues to do for us.

But the upside is that Jesus in His unlimited mercy makes concession for us. His love is not based on our love; it's based on the view he has from His immeasurable dimension of love. He sees us through the eyes of what we can become, and He knows us. Knowing that fills our hearts with hope and renewed faith. A true *hidden treasure*.

We have a powerful and merciful God. He knows we have all fallen short of His glory, but His mercy is incredible. That is why Christians need to always be aware of His love and His mercy. A day shouldn't go by without us praising God. We may be barely able to comprehend His mercy, but we know that it is there. The Bible describes God's mercy and grace in several scriptures. You can read Bible verses about mercy to help guide you on your path. Christian mercy can sometimes be hard to keep, but after reading scripture on mercy, you will become a better Christian.

Psalms 86:5, "For you, Lord, are good, and ready to forgive; and plenteous in mercy to all them that call on you."

Psalms 145:9, "The LORD is good to all: and his tender mercies are over all his works."

Luke 6:36, "Be you therefore merciful, as your Father also is merciful."

Ephesians 2:4, "But God, who is rich in mercy, for his great love with which he loved us."

Titus 3:5, "Not by works of righteousness which we have done, but according to his mercy he saved us, by the washing of regeneration, and renewing of the Holy Ghost."

Hebrews 4:16, "Let us therefore come boldly to the throne of grace, that we may obtain mercy, and find grace to help in time of need."

1 Peter 1:3, "Blessed be the God and Father of our Lord Jesus Christ, which according to his abundant mercy has begotten us again to a lively hope by the resurrection of Jesus Christ from the dead."

> The next morning, the older leaders of the people, the leading priests, and the teachers of the law came together. They led Jesus away to their high council. They said, "If you are the Messiah, then tell us that you are."
>
> Jesus said to them, "If I tell you I am the Messiah, you will not believe me. And if I ask you, you will not answer. But beginning now, the Son of Man will sit at the right side of God All-Powerful." (Luke 22:66–69)

(LP) Beginning Now: A Very Present Mantra

What a prediction and a statement we all can learn from, especially "beginning now," which should be announced from our spirit when in the face of danger and distraction. Say it out loud, "Beginning now!" It resets our call to action in our designated areas and plants our feet more solidly on the path of our destiny. *Beginning now* creates in me a clean heart and renews a right Spirit within me. "A lamp to my feet, a light to my path" "A tree planted by the rivers of water, bring forth fruit in its season." *Beginning now!*

During the writing of this book, we are entering spring and the possibilities are endless as to what the future holds. I stand ready to accomplish all that you desire, Lord, "beginning now"! "The glory of this present house will be greater, than that of the former. And in this place, there will be peace." May I never forget your word and its unstoppable, unshakable promises. Unlimited power behind me and unstoppable possibilities and dimensions before me. *Beginning now!* Uncover all the *hidden treasures in the field.*

Luke 23

The leading priests and teachers of the law were standing there shouting things against Jesus. Then Herod and his soldiers laughed at him. They made fun of him by dressing him in clothes like kings wear. Then Herod sent him back to Pilate. In the past Pilate and Herod had always been enemies. But on that day they became friends.

—Luke 23:10–12

(LP) A Bridge Not Made with Hands

How two uncooperative leaders could became friends, only Jesus could do something like that, right? Like our president and the presidents of other controversial nations. Jesus is a fixer and a true common denominator. There is no telling where seeds of our outreaches may land. It may land in the heart of an unlikely opponent or former enemy. When I see a scripture like this one, that's when I hold out hope against hope that the one I'm praying for with such a resistant attitude can change. I pray a *hidden treasure* will be unveiled across the line of divide! And *a bridge will form not made with hands.*

> But the people continued to shout. They demanded that Jesus be killed on a cross. Their shouting got so loud that Pilate decided to give them what they wanted. They wanted Barabbas to go free—the one who was in jail for starting a riot and for murder. Pilate let Barabbas go free.

> And he handed Jesus over to be killed. This is what the people wanted. (Luke 23:23–25)

(LP) Shout Even Louder

I know this is not the bigger issue here, but there is strength in numbers, especially if everybody is in one accord concerning a subject matter they want to get heard. I don't agree with how some of the protest are being handled, being violent and all, but the loudness of their voices is bringing awareness.

As stated above, I think some of our policies and laws are just the shout of bullies. What we need to do is *shout even louder* in our circle of influence, make a noise that will reverberate around the world. But I think what happens is that Jesus brings us so much peace that our *shout* has got to be in our prayer time our unity and our examples of a better lifestyle. I also pray that a quiet storm will arise from our legal department and spread through the hearts on the hill. Once they side with the true Source, who is our matchless Savior, I believe that the tide will start to turn toward a more civil world again. A world that cares about others as much as we care about ourselves. Shout it to the heavens and watch the *hidden treasures* come raining down!

> A large crowd followed Jesus. Some of the women were sad and crying. They felt sorry for him. But Jesus turned and said to the women, "Women of Jerusalem, don't cry for me. Cry for yourselves and for your children too. The time is coming when people will say, 'The women who cannot have babies are the ones God has blessed. It's really a blessing that they have no children to care for.' Then the people will say to the mountains, 'Fall on us!' They will say to the hills, 'Cover us!' If this can happen to someone who is good, what will happen to those who are guilty?" (Luke 23:27–30)

(LP) Cry…For Your Children

Here it is again, from the mouth of J. C., "*Cry…for your children.*" It is and continues to be an ongoing dilemma in our world. Children getting trashed by evil forces. The more we shine the light on areas they struggle with, it will get increasingly harder for darkness to get a permanent foothold. Also "if this can happen to someone who is good, what will happen to those who are guilty." This phrase is hard to hear, but sometimes good people get swept away with the bad, and there is no answer except that God has a plan—and we, who are called after His name, trust that plan.

> "There were also two criminals led out with Jesus to be killed. They were led to a place called The Skull. There the soldiers nailed Jesus to the cross. They also nailed the criminals to crosses beside Jesus—one on the right and the other on the left" (Luke 23:32–33).

(LP) The Hill of the Skull

Two observations right away: The skull is a popular image for T-shirts, jackets, hats, and other apparel. Now I see that in a different light. I know it is capitalized on from the dark side and maybe it was motivated from there, but it's a great reminder of the ground Jesus died on. Another observation is, Jesus dying between two thieves. In a sense it's Jesus dying right next to us every time we sin. To think of it that way, encourages me to turn away from my willful sins. A day-to-day *hidden treasure.*

> Jesus said, "Father, forgive them. They don't know what they are doing."
> The soldiers threw dice to divide Jesus' clothes between them. The people stood there watching everything. The Jewish leaders laughed at Jesus. They said, "If he is God's Chosen One,

the Messiah, then let him save himself. He saved others, didn't he?"

Even the soldiers laughed at Jesus and made fun of him. They came and offered him some sour wine. They said, "If you are the king of the Jews, save yourself!" (At the top of the cross these words were written: "this is the king of the Jews.") (Luke 23: 43–38)

(LP) What a Heart of Love

What a heart of love that would allow His own creation to laugh and mock Him. It's the same, in our walk sometimes. People will mock us when we mention the name of Jesus and His claims. I don't know about you, but in some cases, I wish the Lord would send them a serious wake-up call. But when a crisis hits their life, guess who they seek out: Jesus and the people who bear his name, *you!*

It's evidenced by the soldiers who represented Rome, which now have become the forefathers of the biggest Christian religion of all time—the Roman Catholic Church. Wrap your head around that one. It's like a *hidden treasure* that God held and then caused to grow over time. That's why I say, you never know who is going to internalize the Gospel. God always does something that we just didn't see coming.

So in the face of obvious rejection, just keep putting one foot in front of the other. Don't give up; don't give in. Even in the face of criticism and sarcasm, you never know how or who will internalize your precious appeal. To the point below:

> One of the criminals hanging there began to shout insults at Jesus: "Aren't you the Messiah? Then save yourself, and save us too!"
>
> But the other criminal stopped him. He said, "You should fear God. All of us will die soon. You and I are guilty. We deserve to die because we did wrong. But this man has done

nothing wrong." Then he said, "Jesus, remember me when you begin ruling as king!"

Then Jesus said to him, "I promise you, today you will be with me in paradise." (Luke 23:39–43)

(LP) "Today You Will be with Me in Paradise"

This scripture again shows that the worse person can have a change of heart, especially when confronted by a circumstance one can't possibly have power over, like death.

It was about noon, but it turned dark throughout the land until three o'clock in the afternoon, because the sun stopped shining. The curtain in the Temple was torn into two pieces. Jesus shouted, "Father, I put my life in your hands!" After Jesus said this, he died.

The army officer there saw what happened. He praised God, saying, "I know this man was a good man!" (Luke 23:44–47)

(LP) No Light, No Life!

What an affect Jesus had on the natural laws of nature. Unexplained occurrences happened. As is with the universe and its origin—unexplained. Some things will be like that, and let the awe set in because there is none like our Lord. Just goes to show, when the light disappears, how chaotic everything becomes. Life loses its value and cohesiveness with the absence of light. That's why God places things in order: to not have fluctuating elements, like gravity. What if all of a sudden gravity fluctuated? A car coming around the corner could start floating, then crashing to the ground. That would be a mess.

The sun gives off light and heat, and we need both to make the earth a warm, comfortable place to live. Plants use light from the sun for photosynthesis, creating food for animals and oxygen for us to breathe. Sunlight makes our days bright, and it reflects off the moon to give us light at night.

Sometimes when I'm on the road at night and have to pull off to get gas, the crickets sound like an orchestra singing to billions of stars in the sky. The awe of God is what needs to be introduced into our busy cities. But unfortunately, there has to be a disaster of some sort to wake us up.

I did notice though that when the pope visited, there was a holy aura accompanying him, in each place he visited. I believe that us saints are projecting something special in our environments as well. It's a *hidden treasure* as we commit ourselves daily like Paul the Apostle. Just our shadow possess God's presence and essences.

> A man named Joseph was there from the Jewish town of Arimathea. He was a good man, who lived the way God wanted. He was waiting for God's kingdom to come. Joseph was a member of the Jewish council. But he did not agree when the other Jewish leaders decided to kill Jesus. He went to Pilate and asked for the body of Jesus. He took the body down from the cross and wrapped it in cloth. Then he put it in a tomb that was dug in a wall of rock. This tomb had never been used before. It was late on Preparation day. When the sun went down, the Sabbath day would begin. (Luke 23:50–54)

(LP) Remember Me?

When a person of influence dies, people can have the same respect for them, as in life. When my mentor and friend Pastor Chuck Smith, founder of the Calvary Chapel Churches, passed away, they had to hold his funeral in an arena. Followers and admirers from all over the country came to pay tribute. I tried to walk through the whole arena to shake hands and thank folks for coming, but I only got a fourth of the way through.

Like Joseph did for Jesus, I believe many will do for you. I'm sure many will get up and share what you meant to them and how their lives were changed because of you. You may not be sent off in an arena, but you will have the arena of many hearts echoing your name for years to come. You are the *hidden treasure* that will continue to live in many hearts.

Luke 24

So the two men got up then and went back to Jerusalem. There they found the followers of Jesus meeting together. The eleven apostles and the people with them said, "The Lord really has risen from death! He appeared to Simon." Then the two men told what had happened on the road. They talked about how they recognized Jesus when he shared the bread with them. While the two men were saying these things to the other followers, Jesus himself came and stood among them. He said to them, "Peace be with you." This surprised the followers. They were afraid. They thought they were seeing a ghost. But Jesus said, "Why are you troubled? Why do you doubt what you see? Look at my hands and my feet. It's really me. Touch me. You can see that I have a living body; a ghost does not have a body like this." After Jesus told them this, he showed them his hands and his feet. The followers were amazed and very, very happy to see that Jesus was alive. They still could not believe what they saw. He said to them, "Do you have any food here?" They gave him a piece of cooked fish. While the followers watched, he took the fish and ate it.

—Luke 24:33–42

(LP) Well, the Physician Did Heal Himself

This passage of scripture is stacked with a-ha moments. A-ha, in verse 39, sounds like Jesus is acknowledging that there are ghosts, of which

I missed that one before. Also, no one had actually seen a person die and then get up and be walking and talking with people. And what kind of body are we going to have after we rise up from the dead? It looks like it's going to be an eating body, hallelujah! And notice it was cooked fish, not sushi. I think that will be negotiable though!

Also the body appears to be physical in nature, not translucent as I always pictured, because it can touch and be touched. It will have emotions, like expressed by our Lord. He really wanted his disciples to be okay with the fact that he was not dead but alive.

In the scriptures prior, Jesus has risen from the dead and it was a rumor among some in the land. But just like Jesus does in our personal relationship experience, you hear about him first, then you have a personal encounter with Him.

So when we go to spread the Word, sometimes it's a seed-planting expedition. But through time, the seeds begin to mature and the person's spirit takes hold of the truth that has been shared.

There are a gang of *hidden treasures* that I never saw or thought about before, which goes to the title of this book *Hidden Treasures in Your Field*. I believe as we go through this life, God will continue to reveal and unveil new sides of himself to us.

Like the song says:

"I serve a risen Savior, He's in the world today...
I know that He is living, whatever men may say.
I see His hand of mercy, I hear His voice of cheer.
And just the time I need Him, He's always near.
He lives, He lives, Christ Jesus lives today.
He walks with me and talks with me, along life's narrow way.
He lives, He lives, salvation to impart.
You ask me how I know He lives...He lives, within, my heart."
(By Alan Jackson)

You are witnesses. You must go and tell people that they must change and turn to God, which will bring them his forgiveness. You must start

from Jerusalem and tell this message in my name
to the people of all nations. Remember that I will
send you the one my Father promised. Stay in the
city until you are given that power from heaven.
(Luke 24:48–49)

(LP) They That Wait Will Mount up with Wings like Eagles!

The Holy Spirit is so important to reinforce us with His power, especially if we are looking to accomplish great things for God. Insights and sensitivities will be given to us, just at the right time— all orchestrated by the Holy Spirit. The key is to *wait* before the Lord in prayer and meditation before our launch. As I mentioned before, I was so ready when I got my call to serve. The Neelys will never know the launching pad they provided when they sought me out some decades ago. It is my honor to serve, but I have to admit, I was anxious to get out here. However, the Lord had me on lockdown before I was released. A lot of praying, Bible study course, Bible studies, counseling sessions, church, mentoring sessions mixed with accountability, to name a few. Preparation was the *hidden treasure* that got me ready for these many happy years of ministry.

"Jesus led his followers out of Jerusalem almost to Bethany. He raised his hands and blessed his followers. While he was blessing them, he was separated from them and carried into heaven. They worshiped him and went back to Jerusalem very happy. They stayed at the Temple all the time, praising God" (Luke 24:50–52).

(LP) Time With You, A New Song

"Time with you, I love spending time with you.
All throughout the day, whether work or play,
You're always on my mind.

Time with you, I love spending time with you.
All throughout the day, I try to find a way,
to make the Son shine."

*I thank our Savior, Jesus Christ for Luke. I hope it has helped
unearth hidden treasures in your field.*

As a bonus, the message about P. U. R. P. O. S. E. starts now:

I know that we have used PURPOSE a lot, over the last decade
or so, but again, I hope this version of it will prove helpful to realign
and fire you up again.

The first two letters stand for—*Pure U.*

There is a certain characteristic as to how God made you that's
different from me or anyone else. As you know from science, that
out of all the billions of people that have lived and will live that each
one has got their own DNA that identifies them. And it started when
you came out of your daddy and went into your mama. Millions of
you were swimming upstream, and you out swam them all! That was
your first sign right there! You…are…special.

Jeremiah 1:5 says, "Before I formed you in the womb I knew
you, and before you were born, I consecrated you; I appointed you a
prophet to the nations."

King David said in Psalm 139:14, "I praise you, for I am fear-
fully and wonderfully made…"

And the big one is out of 1 Corinthians 12:18–30. "But as it
is, God arranged the members in the body each one of them, as he
chose. If all were a single member, where would the body be? As it is,
there are many parts, yet one body. The eye cannot say to the hand,
I have no need of you, nor again the head to the feet, I have no need
of you. On the contrary, the parts of the body that seem to be weaker
are—indispensable.

Genesis 12:2 gives us a great motivation: "And I will make of
you a great nation, and I will bless you and make your name great, so
that you will be a blessing."

Say it out loud—a part of PURPOSE is to be Pure U.

As I grab an ember from my past, I think back to a time when
I was eight at my Mama Doll's Baptist church. The music direc-

tor and the whole church would enjoy me singing the Lord's Prayer. Some Sundays they would put me on a box and have me sing it acapella. One Sunday I can remember Pastor Haynes prophesying that I would be in ministry one day.

And here I am writing to you, memoirs from that life that was prophesied to me—talking and singing and being fired up from that ember from my past. I think of all the nightclubs and special social groups I played for. Then the great honor of a music career that certified me as a professional, with Santana. Then the call to salvation and the many thousands of souls, maybe even millions, saved, on their way to heaven. And all the many experiences God used to make me have the flavor I have.

Well, I'm sure we each have stories to tell of how we became who we've become. But that's the Pure U—God is using to accomplish his call. It's like Joseph and his administrative gift that helped him administrate Potiphar's household, and then a jail, to finally being noticed by the highest power in the land at that time, which ultimately lead him to become vice president of Egypt.

So we thank God for this individual flavor of ours. It's just as important to our purpose as anything else.

Say it out loud—Pure U is important to His Purpose.

RP stands for *Reflecting Pops*.

I believe if we're really reflecting Pops, His Glory should emanate from us. The greatest compliment someone can pay you is when they say, "When you come into a room, the room changes" or "You remind me of your daddy!"

The scriptures that are in 1 Kings 8 really give a good picture of *Reflecting Pops*. Do you remember the story of King Solomon building the temple and putting the sacred articles in the Holy Place? What's especially interesting is when the priest put down the ark with the two tablets in it, under the wings of the cherub. As they left the room, Scripture says, "When the priests came out of the Holy Place, the cloud filled the Lord's Temple. The priests could not continue their work because the Temple was filled with the Glory of the Lord."

That, I believe is a direct depiction of us. That as we recount the promises, the times when God has been faithful to us, the prophesies that have been spoken over our lives, it's just like the sacred articles being put in the Holy Place. God's glory just begins to emanate from us, each ember from the past *Reflecting Pops*.

I don't know about you, but when I start to talk about God's goodness, I feel like a little kid again because there was a time in my life when I believed Him wholeheartedly like a little child. And I must admit, sometimes being grown-up and mature is not all that much fun—it makes me have to do too much thinking. What does that comedian say, "Get her done!" At the Lazarus tomb didn't Jesus say, "Did I not say to you, that if you believe, you will see the glory of God" (John 11:40).

Say it out loud—my purpose is Reflecting Pops.

The *O* stands for *Reflecting Pop's Optimism.*

Someone who is optimistic is hopeful about the future. In other words, looking on the bright side of things.

So you need a few Bible verses out of Scriptures, do ya! No problem. I think Psalms 23 encompasses all the emotions we go through as leaders and lay people and is very optimistic!

The LORD *is* my shepherd; I shall not want.

2   He maketh me to lie down in green pastures:
     He leadeth me beside the still waters.

3   He restoreth my soul:
     He leadeth me in the paths of righteousness for his name's sake.

4   Yea, though I walk through the valley of the shadow of death,
     I will fear no evil: for thou *art* with me;
   thy rod and thy staff they comfort me.

5   Thou preparest a table before me in the presence of mine enemies:
     thou anointest my head with oil;
   my cup runneth over.

6   Surely goodness and mercy shall follow me all the days of my life:
     and I will dwell in the house of the LORD for ever.

That's reflecting Pop's Optimism.

Of course, you know the story of me going from Santana to Hosanna right? I had no idea what was in store for my future, but I kept being guided by His word, which made me optimistic!

Say it out loud—my purpose is reflecting Pop's Optimism!

The *S* stands for *(Reflecting Pop's) Stamina.*

Stamina to me means having hope for the hopeless. Stamina is continued prayer. When a husband has gone astray, when a wife has let a wayward woman at work pull her away from her morals and family commitments, we continue to believe that the weapons of our warfare are not carnal but mighty through God, to the pulling down of strongholds, casting down imagination, and every high thing that would exalt itself against the knowledge of God. Bringing into captivity every thought to the obedience of Christ. That's stamina.

I don't know if you've seen the movie *The War Room* but it's all about *(Reflecting Pop's) Stamina.* First of all, when I went to the movie theater to see it, it was the most enjoyable experience partially because we have a new theater in town where you could put your feet up like you do at home. Also it was enjoyable, from the language angle, with no cussing. Another emotion was eating popcorn and wiping tears. The movie over all was so refreshing. I need to re-watch it to remind myself of how to stand in face of things at home that test my stamina.

The word PURPOSE it just a tool to use for realignment.

Say it out loud—I really Reflect Pop's Stamina.

And the last letter is *E*, which stands of *(Reflecting Pop's) Essence,* which I believe is at God's core because it's all about His essence.

We can learn many things about our God, even on a scholar level. But the essence comes from being with Him. And if we as leaders are the translators of our precious Lord, His essence should be reflected.

Scriptures say in Colossians 1:15–20,

> He is the image of the invisible God, the firstborn
> of all creation. For by Him all things were created,
> both in the heavens and on earth, visible and invis-

ible, whether thrones or dominions or rulers or authorities—all things have been created through Him and for Him. He is before all things, and in Him all things hold together. He is also head of the body, the church; and He is the beginning, the firstborn from the dead, so that He Himself will come to have first place in everything. For it was the Father's good pleasure for all the fullness to dwell in Him, and through Him to re-con-cile all things to Himself, having made peace through the blood of His cross; through Him, I say, whether things on earth or things in heaven.

So as leaders, the more investment we make in Christ, the more of His essence is revealed in us.

Say it out loud—I am full of God's Essence!

Example: I was ministering in Rancho Mirage recently, and my prayer starting this year was to have 10 percent more of God's anointing than the concert before. Between service I went into the public bathroom, and a guy was crying.

I said, "What's up, my friend?"

He said, "From the moment you came on stage, I started crying uncontrollably. I just don't understand it."

I explained my prayer about the 10 percent more anointing, but it didn't quite connect with him, so he kept shaking his head as he left the bathroom. For me, I was thanking God because I knew His Essence was being transferred.

This is what we all pray for: that Pop's essence can be pulled out of Scripture when we study, out of our prayer lives, out of song, a poem.

When you need realignment, let PURPOSE help you reach back and grab an ember from your childlike beginnings: Pure U-Reflecting Pop's Optimism-Stamina-Essence.

And as God's glory shines bright in us, we will issue an alert in our various circles that God is calling for a mass recall and it starts with us first.

Listen to how King Solomon put it in 1 Kings 8:22–24:

> Then Solomon stood in front of the whole assembly of Israel and faced the Lord's altar. Solomon spread his hands and looked toward heaven and said, "Lord, God of Israel, there is no other god like you in heaven or on the earth. You keep the agreement that you made with your people. You are kind and loyal to those who follow you with all their heart. You made a promise to your servant, my father David, and you kept that promise. You made that promise with your own mouth, and with your own hands you made it come true today."

Another passages shows the mass recall of that day, starting in verse 33.

> Sometimes your people Israel will sin against you, and their enemies will defeat them. Then the people will come back to you and praise you. They will pray to you in this Temple. Please listen in heaven, please listen to the prayers of your people Israel. Forgive them for their sins and let them have their land again. You gave this land to their ancestors.
>
> Sometimes they will sin against you, and you will stop the rain from falling on their land. Then they will pray toward this place and praise your name. You make them suffer, and they will be sorry for their sins. So please listen in heaven to their prayer. Then forgive us for our sins. Teach the people to live right. Then, Lord, please send rain to the land you gave them.

Then this last scripture is for the world mass recall:

> People from other places will hear about your
> greatness and your power. They will come from
> far away to pray at this Temple. From your home
> in heaven, please listen to their prayers. Please do
> everything the people from other places ask you.
> Then they will fear and respect you the same as
> your people in Israel. Then all people everywhere
> will know that I built this Temple to honor you.
> (vs. 41–43)

Yeah, finished!

God's PURPOSE for LP in a nutshell.

The part I play is in "new exploration," which always is a position of trying to get along with everybody, experiencing acceptance in whatever venue of life I find myself in.

In '74 when I rededicated my life back to Jesus. I was introduced to the Assembly of God denomination. I had never heard of this group because I was raised mainly Baptist and Methodist, with a little Catholic altar boy experience, which, according to what I do today, was all a set up.

I continued with my secular carrier at the time with Carlos Santana and expressed my new faith in the entertainment industry. As stated in this book, a whole world of new beginnings was being asked of me. To stand out in my environment and effect change in the hearts of us mostly narcissistic ego-driven people and announce to them to put Jesus instead of themselves on the top shelf of their life. Of course, this was not a popular suggestion at the time. But that's what the Lord was asking of me.

Then the rubber meeting the road experience came in the form of changing my career altogether and joining with a few other musicians that were taking the same challenge. On the West Coast, my first introduction to any outlet along those lines was Lewis and Mary Neely, pastors of Warehouse Ministries, out of Sacramento, California. In turn they introduced me to Pastor Chuck Smith, CEO of the Calvary Chapel Denomination. At the time of our meeting they had just formed a record label for the express purpose of distributing this new style music called contemporary Christian music headed by Pastor Chucks nephew, Chuck Fromm.

The formulation of Maranatha Music was off and running but had limited distribution and radio airplay opportunity. So Chuck Fromm got a hold of Stan Moser, VP of Word Records, out of Waco, Texas. If was a match made in heaven because they had a lot of reach in the industry but no artist quite like me from the secular crossover world.

During this tremendous time of *new exploration*, I must have been a part of every denomination on the planet. Even getting the opportunity to be the advance artist and participating in the Crusades of Dr. Billy Graham. This too was an eye-opening experience, culturally. Because even though I had a Baptist experience, it was seen through a Black Baptist community with a certain language, food and, culture all unto itself. The stretch was to adapt to this new language, foods, slang, and jokes in a Caucasian community.

Wasn't long after that, that I went full time into my own ministry, dragging huge amounts of gear, trucks, and motorhomes behind me. It was a one-man show but required the same look and sound as the big bands. It required being on the road twenty days out of the month and not much downtime because crew was also depending on these concerts for their livelihood.

Then comes an absolute burnout in '88 that I never thought could happen to me, which took two years and a lot of counseling to bounce back from. During my much-needed time off, I kept hearing the words, "And Foreigners will rebuild your walls." And it all came true, that my first concerts back were in Russia, followed four years later by meeting a Filipino lady on a cruise, who would become my wife.

A truly *new exploration* occurred in '91 with the *Leon and Friends* show, Saturday nights on TBN. All my friends that were converted secular artist came on the show to sing and give their testimonies. Even though I had never hosted before, it ended up being a top-ten rated show.

In '98 I got the urge to start a church in Long Beach called The Rock House. At the time I was concerned about doing too many concerts again and decided this would be a good way to minister to people without having to tour twenty days out of the month, to create a community of believers that could affect Long Beach, LA, and, eventually, greater California. I didn't realize that one has to be called to this sort of work. I thought you just make a decision to do something and just put on different shoes. Well, as time let me know, those shoes fit like ski boats. As a man used for a global initiative, I felt like I was hiding from my true call.

In 1999, a *new exploration.* Peter Lowe had begun his Get Motivated Seminars with such guests as Colin Powell, Michael Phelps, Mayor Giuliani, foreign dignitaries, and former presidents from all over the world, sharing their stories of success and ideas of how all the attendees could accomplish their dreams. And guess who Peter chose to be the music artist for this great outreach to the financial community? Yep, yours truly.

It ended in 2012 while we had already started our retirement program. But in our new city, there seemed to be more needs that our specific calling couldn't resist. So we jumped in with both feet to help the youngsters in our town.

In 2016 we were made aware of Kangen Alkalized Water, and we have form a club called *The Life Changers Club*. CLUB standing for "Christ Leads Us Best." It was started with the idea of helping those we love to drink the best water for their hydration and degenerate diseases. It has provided a great maintenance plan, because as you know, we, especially in the body of Christ, pray for healing, like say diabetes. Then after we're healed, we run right out to Krispy Kreme doughnuts. The temple is important and vital to us feeling motivated to "go ye therefore and teach all nations…" And Renee has added a new wing to our ministry called Advancing Together. It allows people to work from home, making unbelievable money from their computer. It's being led by a group of Digital Geniuses that are half our age. But it's helping a lot of my fans worldwide upgrade their income to six and seven figures in some cases, www.*AdvancingTogether.online*.

In this present moment we are preparing for an inspirational show on the strip here in Las Vegas in the Leon Patillo Sanctuary and excited about the release of my first book.

Thanks for reading it, and I hope you enjoy the music too!

Blessings, blessings,
Leon

About the Author

Leon Patillo has been a musical icon and musical force as lead vocalist for the Hall of Fame group Santana. His roots in Christ stem back to childhood but became fully activated in 1974 through the help of a girlfriend's brother.

He was one of the artist instrumental in the development of contemporary Christian music. A style at the time that first appealed to a young audience but later grew to include a full-age range.

Leon's first solo release was *Dance Children Dance*, an album of which he wrote, produced, sang, arranged the horns and string parts, and played all the basic instruments. Subsequently Leon went on to write and produce seven other albums through the Word/Warner affiliate labels.

Hidden Treasures in Your Field is the first book written by Leon Patillo. He says that it was inspired by his personal studies in the book of Luke. Leon goes on to say that he was looking for one resounding theme that wove through the book but discovered that there were many, many themes just below the surface, thus the title of this book.

Leon still performs all over the world and mentors talented children who need guidance in their art and in their life direction. Leon is the father of six children, eighteen grandchildren, and three great-grandchildren and husband to his lovely Filipino wife, Renee. This book is designed to inspire the reader to uncover some usable gems for personal confidence and to brighten up God's purpose for your life. Leon calls this a book of memoirs.

Leon Patillo is proudly sponsored by Subaru of Las Vegas.

CPSIA information can be obtained
at www.ICGtesting.com
Printed in the USA
FSHW011128270821
84025FS

9 781644 587584